CRISIS

AND

COMEBACK

CORK

IN THE EIGHTIES

MICHAEL MOYNIHAN is a journalist with the *Irish Examiner*. He has also written for RTÉ, Today FM, *The Observer* and the *Washington Post*. He was born and raised in Cork, where he lives with his wife and two children. He is the author of several successful books and has twice been shortlisted for Sports Book of the Year.

 facebook.com/michael.moynihan.54

 @MikeMoynihanEx

For Donal and Mary, Marjorie, Clara and Bridget.

CRISIS
AND
COMEBACK

IN THE EIGHTIES

MICHAEL MOYNIHAN

The Collins Press

First published in 2018 by
The Collins Press
West Link Park
Doughcloyne
Wilton
Cork
T12 N5EF
Ireland

Paperback ISBN: 978-1-84889-356-6

Typesetting by Carrigboy Typesetting Services
Typeset in Garamond
Printed in Poland by Drukarnia Skleniarz

Contents

Introduction

It was a different city then. Coming out of the 1970s, Cork's swagger was intact, its position in the world secure. The previous ten years had been dominated nationally by its favourite son, who was Taoiseach for much of the decade, and the sense of superiority was not confined to the political arena.

The city had given Ireland a genuine, world-class music star and boasted one of the first officially licensed, internationally recognised film festivals, which had been on the road since the 1950s and had attendance in the thousands at its peak. Cork had produced the country's first modern GAA superstar earlier in the decade and at times in the 1970s there were not one but two League of Ireland football clubs in the city.

Cork bustled: people came to the centre of the city to shop and socialise, to visit the same places their parents had visited for years. St Patrick's Street on a Saturday afternoon heaved with people shopping in Roches Stores and Cash's; they took the kids into Mandy's or Burgerland as a treat afterwards.

They read the *Cork Examiner* and *Evening Echo* over Barry's tea and cakes made in Thompson's bakery, in Mary Rose's coffee shop in the Queen's Old Castle or the Green Door on Academy Street.

On a Saturday night Patrick Street heaved as well: people streamed into the centre of the city from the northern and southern suburbs. The bars and clubs rocked every autumn with the newly created Jazz Festival, which quickly established its primacy as the go-to destination every October bank holiday. They went to the movies in the Pavilion, the Capitol, the Cameo, the Lee and other cinemas.

There was a stability to the city, and key to that stability were the institutions which anchored the city and reinforced its identity: the English Market, still trading after almost two centuries; the university, slightly stand-offish on the Western Road, and the regional technical college further out; the two breweries, on opposite sides of the river, Murphy's and Beamish.

Underpinning those were key employers, significant industries such as Ford, Dunlop and Verolme, which were internationally recognised names, deeply rooted in the fabric of the city and county after decades of employing the natives. Of the three factories, there was no doubt which was the pre-eminent employer. Dunlop employed 1,800 people there at its peak, and there was a prestigious international element to shipbuilding, but Ford was first among equals, a tangible marker of quality. Tyres were necessary but unglamorous, and nobody had a naval frigate in their driveway. A Ford car, however, was a product any worker would be proud of, and there had been a time when 7,000 people earned a living in its Cork base.

The work somewhere like the mould room in Dunlop could be hot and dirty. Verolme had a significant Dutch element – a management cohort who kept their distance from staff for the most part. Ford, however, was deeply rooted across the culture in Cork. The Ford boxes became part of local folklore, the sturdy packing crates in which parts for the factory arrived. These provided the raw material for garden sheds all over the city and makeshift beachside chalets, while a factory soccer team, Fordsons, became FAI Cup champions in 1926.

The Dunlop social club on the Blackrock Road provided an outlet for thousands over the years, but the grip Ford exerted was visible in a *Sunday Times* interview with Jack Lynch in the early 1970s. The then-leader of the opposition drove a Ford, the journalist noted, out of loyalty to the firm that employed so many of his constituents. (These loyalties counted. When another Cork politician, Michael O'Leary, visited Dunlop, the workers noted his tyres were Semperit rather than the local brand.)

Ford was famously described as a Cork firm with an American branch, a joke that not only underlined the strength of the links between the city and the home office in Dearborn, but offered a telling insight into the city's trust in the company.

This, then, was the city: confident and busy, and apparently bucking the trends of the late 1970s, as the ripples of the oil crisis spread economic uncertainty across the globe. Cork was seen as an exception to the malaise. The city featured, famously, on the cover of *Business & Finance* in October 1980. The headline said everything you needed to know. 'Cork: What Recession?'

Halfway through the 1980s, however, Cork was in chaos. Ford, Dunlop and Verolme all closed within eighteen months of each other, and every institution in the city seemed under threat. The North Infirmary hospital closed. Murphy's Brewery almost shut down early in the decade and Beamish & Crawford faced its own survival crisis later in the 1980s. There were rumours that Cork Airport itself was in the firing line. The English Market survived not one but two devastating fires, only for Cork Corporation to strongly consider turning the Market into a multistorey car park.

The uncertainty spread beyond the unemployment statistics, horrific though those were. There was an outbreak of joyriding in the city, disaffected youths stealing cars and leading gardaí on high-speed chases to nowhere, a vivid illustration of the despair in the city. An illiterate sandwich-board carrier was elected to the corporation. People in Cork claimed to see religious statues moving.

The film festival was broke and trying to hang on to its one asset, the projector. There was no League of Ireland team at all in the city for a couple of seasons, and in the same years the county hurlers lost two consecutive All-Ireland finals.

In an effort to bolster spirit in the city a festival was launched to commemorate the granting of a Royal Charter eight centuries before, the Cork 800. It was supposed to begin with an air show at Cork Airport but that had to be cancelled. It was too foggy for the airplanes.

How did Cork turn things around? Some crucial decisions were made, such as backing an obscure American company's plans to locate a factory on the city's north side, long before it became one of the richest companies in the history of the world.

A new microelectronics centre opened near the university, bolstering the city's reputation as modern, technologically savvy, and open for business. An academic's parting words with an entrepreneur getting into his car led to another key industry coming to the city. After years of neglect the cityscape improved. The English Market survived. League of Ireland football returned. The hurlers started to win All-Irelands again. The film festival was rescued.

The lessons were taught in a hard school, as the poet Theo Dorgan put it, but they were learned. There was no other choice.

1

Market or Car Park?

The English Market's experience of the 1980s is emblematic of the city, fittingly enough, as few other institutions are as closely identified with the city as the Market. The fact that it managed to survive, unlike other long-standing institutions, would be worth underlining in and of itself, but the manner of its survival makes it all the more relevant.

In latter years the Market has become synonymous with the city, or more synonymous than ever before – visiting film crews inevitably capture footage of the crowded walkways between stalls bursting with fresh produce, while tourists seeking an authentic Cork experience share those winding passages with locals shopping for groceries where their parents and grandparents strolled in their own time. The high-water mark of its status as an integral part of Cork's identity came in 2011, when Queen Elizabeth II of England visited the Market and laughed along with stallholders.

The pomp and ceremony of a royal visit seemed apposite, given the problems the Market had faced down in its time.

Founded in 1788, it had survived challenges as ferocious as the Great Famine and revolution, and as mundane as out-of-town shopping centres, coming through to surf the more recent wave of interest in traceable food and environmentally friendly producers. Why then did the corporation want to replace it with a car park in the 1980s?

Go back to the start of that decade, and the phone call which woke up the O'Connell family early one morning. At a time when mobile messaging and social media were far in the future, hearing the jangle of a landline telephone at six o'clock in the morning usually meant bad news. That was Pat O'Connell's thinking when the phone rang, and he wasn't wrong.

'I remember the phone going off in the hall that early in the morning, and my mother letting a screech out of her when she answered it. Obviously bad news, a call at that time of the morning, though we were early risers anyway.'

It was 30 June 1980. O'Connell's mother had been told about a fire in the Market, where the family fish stall was under threat.

'We all hopped into the van and headed in, and we were absolutely devastated when we saw the fire. It was probably more devastating than a death in the family because we were so entwined with the Market, to be honest. It was part of our lives and suddenly all we could see was smoke billowing out of the Prince's Street entrance. We managed to get into our own stall but we could see the devastation. The fountain was in the middle of it and all you could hope, really, was that that was going to be the phoenix coming out of the ashes, but there were no guarantees. It was strange to be looking at the sky where there had been a roof.'

Six units of the Cork City Fire Brigade had to cut their way through the metal gates barring the entrance in order to fight the fire. Their priority was to cut off the gas supply. The firemen needed to access the balcony overlooking the fountain area, which they did, and they were thus able to contain the fire and prevent it from spreading to the Grand Parade end. Within half an hour they had brought the fire under control, but eleven stalls had been destroyed.

Later on, firefighters picking their way through the charred, smoking rubble were fearful that the ornate wrought-iron fountain at the Prince's Street entrance had been destroyed, and they found a mass of debris there. Underneath the rubbish, though, the fountain was intact. The metal was till hot to the touch, one of the firemen would later recall, but it had survived.

The Market would be rebuilt – the cost of £300,000 was a significant amount at the time – but O'Connell remembers the early 1980s as a grim period in its history.

'The Market wasn't doing brilliantly that time anyway. It's always easy to be wise in hindsight, but the signs were there that things were beginning to slip a bit, if you had your eyes open. For instance, there were too many butchers in the Market at that time and the competition between them was ferocious – it was a race to the bottom when you look back on it, because if Tommy was giving three chops for a pound, then Jimmy next door to him would try to give four for a pound. Every stallholder became obsessed with the internal competition rather than what was happening in food retail in general. Price became more important than quality.

'The result of that was always going to be the quality going down and down. The Market has always prided itself on keeping in the middle of the top end, if you like; we rely on local produce and we have a job, promoting food in Cork. We all realise that and take it very seriously even if we don't shout and roar about it. We take a pride in our local food sources, and with the connections to restaurants in terms of supplying them you get a feel for what's going on. At the time you're probably too close to it, really, you can't see the wood for the trees, but looking back now … no. The signs weren't good.'

In that sense the Market was collateral damage in the growth of the city, which had been expanding outwards. Shopping centres were located on the periphery of the city, drawing people out of the city or, more likely, encouraging those living in the suburbs to abandon the traditional excursion to town for their weekly shopping. In time, those shopping centres in Ballyvolane, Wilton and Douglas, combined with a pre-existing slight drop in footfall 'probably started to kick a little bit, all right' says O'Connell: 'But we didn't have a culture of it until then. Ballyvolane was the first to hit the city centre because Dunnes Stores was up there, and it was probably a little bit out of town compared to other places.

'You were beginning to notice that Mrs Murphy wasn't coming in once a week any more. Now she was coming in every second week or third week. We felt first that it was a novelty, that people would come back to the Market, and that happened, all right – even if people were doing a weekly shop in one of the shopping centres they still tended to come in for their meat, their fish and so on.

'But when Douglas Court opened we opened a small unit there to hedge our bets at the same time. The trouble was we were paying as much for a tiny unit out there as we were for two or three units in the Market. There isn't a large margin in food anyway so you'll suffer if you're selling one product – fish or meat – in a centre like that, given the costs.'

Then there was the plan to get rid of the Market as we know it. This proposal would gain momentum later in the decade, around

1988, after the loss of thousands of jobs, when the short-term boost in revenue for the Corporation would have been appealing. In O'Connell's words, the plans were 'scarily serious'. The specifics involved a multistorey car park above the market space.

'This was a time when multistorey car parks were supposed to solve all problems in cities. I think Sean Beausang of the Corporation had been over to Wales – Swansea – where there was a market with a car park over it and the bus station next to it. I don't know if there was an original market there, I suspect there was, but this was a "modern" market, and he felt that was the way to go – to knock what we had, put the traders over in the Coal Quay for the couple of years there'd be building. Then they'd all come back to nice new modern stalls, with a multistorey car park overhead.

'It would never have worked. It would have been absolutely insane. And it was the women in here who said, "that isn't happening, lads".'

Nowadays the preponderance of women among the stallholders is striking in the English Market, and in the 1980s it was the central group of female stallholders who held the line in the face of the corporation's plans.

'Among them were my own mother, Eileen Ahern below and Siobhan, Mrs McDonnell, Mrs O'Sullivan,' says O'Connell. 'They were tough ladies, really tough, and they said, "that's not what the Market is. It's in trouble but it's been here since 1790 and survived famines and fires, it'll survive this if we pull together, if we have that passion about us."

'I think everybody had been so shocked by what had happened in the city that they'd recoiled into themselves a little, but then they realised, "our predecessors came through tough times, we can do it." That hard core of people saved the Market, I think. The traders' committee went knocking on every councillor's door and said it wasn't a good idea.'

15

To convince the councillors the traders' committee had to make some points about the modern retail experience, but they also had to convey the essence of the market experience: what differentiates a place like the English Market from other shops, other places.

'They pointed out that if you closed the Market for two years, it'd be a disaster. People change their shopping habits and other businesses step in and take over, obviously. We got over it but I think it also showed how careful you have to be with something like the Market. If it's gone, it's gone.

'Not everyone understands a market, how it works, the balance that's involved. A market has to be rooted in tradition, and ours is very much family-oriented and generational. If you break that link then it's hard to restore, you're going back to start from scratch. But it can't be a museum either, some place where you come in and watch old trades performed for you. It has to trade and it has to make money, to employ people, all of that.

'And we're lucky with the Market that we've always had the core of seven or eight people who understand it, who understand that we're only passing through and that it's important to keep it for the next generation, that we leave it to them in a strong situation. We're lucky in the Market that people have come through and stood up on occasions when they're needed – such as when the idea of a multistorey market was mentioned.'

It seems difficult to conceive of now – brutalist concrete hiding parking spaces instead of the ornate iron gates at the Grand Parade and Prince's Street entrances – but part of that may be the Market's current status as one of Cork's biggest tourist draws. In the 1980s, when the city was struggling, all options were on the table. Thousands of jobs had vanished and the Market was suffering as much as any other sector. O'Connell remembers the closures of Ford, Dunlop and Verolme and the impact they had.

'Oh Jesus, yes. Those job losses devastated the city, it was as bad a period in Cork's history as I've seen. Great employers, and then the peripheral industries that fed off them ... they also seemed to go suddenly. I know there was talk about it but people didn't really believe it could happen. They'd been in Cork for so long, they were engrained in the culture of the city, and people believed it just wouldn't happen.

'It was shock, pure and simple. Everybody knew somebody working there, and the sense was "this couldn't happen". But it did. The Market was absolutely hammered by the closures. Hammered. It depends on local people, and not only were those local people out of pocket, there was a sense of depression over the city, there was a sense of horror there. The sense was "if we can't hold these industries, our biggest, what chance do we have of attracting in new ones?"'

When that initial shock dissipated, O'Connell reckons it took time – 'two or three years' – to readjust to the new reality.

'That people wouldn't just arrive in Cork and love the place and set up businesses here. People realised there were economics involved, that the city had to box smarter to attract those industries and employers. We're very parochial. We thought Ford was Irish – that it was a Cork business, not an Irish business – and we had so many families like the Dwyers and the Barrys who were smart business people, who created a lot of employment, that we felt insulated from things like that.

'It was the first time we saw multinationals in operation, that sentiment didn't come into it when it came to these kinds of decisions. They liked Cork, but ... and that "but" came in capital letters. I think it took those few years for people to

17

adjust, and it was Apple which helped people to do that, which taught people that we had to be smarter in terms of jobs.

'The whole Market reflected that gloom, that depression. At the time, in the 1980s, there were thirteen or fourteen stalls empty – that was one of the reasons we expanded, though everybody laughed when we did that. My mother invested about £40,000 at the time into opening a second stall when most of the stalls around us were closed or closing. We were thinking, "is this clever?", but we rode it out, and when things turned we were ready for it, then.'

Riding it out meant defeating that plan to put a multistorey car park over the stalls.

'It's very hard to credit now, to envisage what would have been put in its place. Because the Market was in trouble at that time, they were looking at alternative businesses, as had happened in Swansea.'

Eventually O'Connell went to see the Welsh model for the new Market himself. Up close, he realised that it was a different proposition entirely.

'It was nothing like what we have here. To me, it's more of a flea market, and that's not an insult, because there's a place for a flea market, but it's not a food market. There's no sense of culture such as you get here. Why do tourists come in here, after all? Because there's a sense of place here, a sense of Cork. We're lucky in that we've managed to keep that sense of place. Obviously, people's shopping habits have changed, and they're shopping online and so on, but we've managed to keep our core customers.

'And a lot of the foreign nationals who work in the likes of Facebook and Apple come in here – and they automatically feel at home. They're used to markets along these lines at home. Funnily enough, you'd often speak to English people when they come in, and they say, "we used to have a market in our town like this but developers bought the site" – because markets tend to be in the centre of towns, obviously. It's valuable property.

'If the local authority doesn't understand that there's a value to a market that goes beyond the commercial value to the area, if they don't see the bigger picture of what it brings to a city in terms of promotion and culture … the council has to understand that, and it can be difficult because often it's not their area of expertise. In a downturn they're under pressure for rates, for instance, to pay for all the services that make a city work.'

O'Connell gives the local authority due credit nowadays, however.

'In fairness, Cork City Council has bought into the sense of what the Market brings. In terms of rent increases they're very realistic – when they compare our rents to Patrick Street, we say that's fine if they want telephone shops in the Market, but they won't have a food market. They have to understand what they have in the Market, and those were discussions which were before the Queen came, by the way, when it wasn't nearly as easy to sell as an idea.

'To me the Coal Quay was another magical place – it was unusual with trees and turkeys at Christmas, but it just slipped through the cracks.'

The demise of the Coal Quay illustrates clearly that the survival of unique locations like the Market is not assured. It takes work, co-operation, understanding: a combination requiring a delicate balance.

'We're lucky at the moment that the Council gets it and understands it. Who's to say that won't change in twenty years' time? Because it took a lot of persuading to stop them from putting up the car park that time. It would have been easy money for the Council, or Corporation, at the time, particularly with the mentality that "we'll always have the Market". But it would have been gone after two years away – people get different habits, they get jobs elsewhere, and the whole thing is different.

'Dublin City Council came down a couple of years ago, they wanted to do a market in Dublin, and they asked if we'd be interested in being involved. We said no, one was enough – but I asked who they were going to get in for the market. They were naming out wholesalers and I was thinking no, they didn't get it. I looked around the Market and saw people involved who were second generation, third generation … this is what they do.

'Of course, they supply restaurants but they're not wholesalers, they're traditional retailers. Mrs Murphy comes in every Friday morning for thirty years and now her daughter is coming in … it's not just bricks and mortar. Instant tradition doesn't work, there isn't the same background in stories built up over the years. One chap from Asia who went to UCC twelve or fourteen years ago came back recently, he came to the stall and asked if I remembered him. "I do actually," I said, "you were a student, weren't you?"

'And he said he was, he'd be down every week to get his fish, and though he was back home in Asia, he still loved Cork – and the fact that he came in and reintroduced himself, I thought that was great, that it showed a real sense of the place.'

O'Connell's view of the Market as a melting pot for new-comers to the city is persuasive: 'Cork people are nosy anyway. They're not afraid to ask where you're from. Cork's shape and size does lend itself to a successful market. When strangers come to the city, the Market is a place where they build up a relationship quickly with the people in the stalls because that's what we do.

'They may not know the fish, or the cuts, and they feel a bit more relaxed because they're dealing with someone who gets what it is they want to do – they don't want to dip the fish in flour and fry it on the pan, they want to steam it in ginger and garlic or whatever. And we chat away and ask them if they're working in Apple or studying in UCC, and straight away they have a connection which they mightn't have made in a bigger city, or in a supermarket.

'The Market has all that, and Cork's a friendly city anyway. People have time to listen in the Market, and if your English isn't good, that's not a problem. When the Spanish come in and ask to have their bass cleaned out they'll say, "can you open it like a book," which isn't the way Irish people say it, but you know immediately what they want. And that relationship starts off because that's what we do.'

The Market is now known all over the world thanks to Queen Elizabeth's visit. O'Connell acknowledges the peak but is always worried about a possible trough following.

'Julian King was the ambassador when the Queen arrived, and a few weeks after the visit he called in to us and said, "the Market really made an impression on her, she's still talking about it."

'And we said that that's what we always do, chat away to people, and he said, "yeah, but people don't usually do that when they meet the Queen of England." It doesn't matter to us if you're royalty or penniless, if you come in to us for fish then you're a customer.

'The visit lifted the profile of the place in terms of tourism. It's given recognition that it's a very special place, the Market, but we've known that for a while without being big-headed. We've stood back and examined why it gets that kind of media attention, and our feeling is that it's unique, it has the friendliness that's been maintained through the generation.

'You go abroad and see how other markets have changed, and while this place has changed too, and modernised – when you look back at the 1960s and see no refrigeration, wallpaper, tarmacadam floors, you'd say, "sweet Jesus, how did we get away with that," but that was the standard of the time.'

And worries?

'Always. Always. The worry is that you won't keep the backbone of family businesses. Food is so streamlined in its delivery … there's only a fraction of the number of butchers that would have been here in the 1950s, and now we have an olive stall and a chocolate stall – things that wouldn't have been thought sustainable years ago, but do you stick rigidly to what you have and fight the tide, or twist a bit? So far we've been lucky, and there is an element of luck involved. Who knows what retail will be like in ten years' time, the way things are changing?

'Wary is probably the word I'd use. We'd be conscious of how things change and we wouldn't want to be the last dinosaurs standing, but we'd like to think it'll survive the next 200 years.'

Still, it wouldn't be the first time an English visitor helped the English Market. Keith Floyd is a key person in the recent history of the Market and central to its success, says O'Connell.

Given the way photogenic cooks now dominate the TV listings, it is difficult to convey the impact someone like Floyd had. His rambling travelogues, interspersed with energetic cooking outbursts and emphatic on-air directions to the camera operator, were compulsive viewing. There was one legendary episode of his show shot in a Welsh rugby club which ended with Floyd, and the contents of a large silver tray of food, on the floor.

He was genuinely passionate about the Market and filmed there often; there is footage in one clip of Floyd talking fish while O'Connell chops and slices in the background.

'He was the original of the species, really, in terms of being a TV chef, but I also think he was one of the first people to spot the potential in the Market, long before anyone else. He was well ahead of people in that regard. He picked up on people's passion for food and also that people were starting to travel, and that food could become part of that travel experience.

'Food tourism was non-existent at the time, but he recognised that there was an incredible food culture in Cork, with the Market the symbol of that, in many ways. But it's the symbol of an awful lot more in the city as well – it reflects the times.'

O'Connell's view of the Market as a canary in the mine for all of Cork is persuasive: 'If Cork is doing well then the Market is doing well, and similarly, if Cork is struggling then the Market is struggling too. You'll see it here, because it depends on local businesses and local people. And that's the magic of the Market, that if you want a feel for Cork there isn't a better place to get that. You walk through and you hear the banter among the stalls, you see the interaction between the customer and the stallholder.

'It gives you a sense of the rivalries, north- and south-side, the sporting clubs people follow, the people from other counties slag you about their teams ... the Market's a small space in the centre of Cork but it's also a barometer for the city.'

That kind of perspective helps with evaluation, of course. Having seen the 1980s up close and personal qualifies O'Connell to point out what made that decade different to the crash following the financial crisis of 2008.

'If we're honest, we all knew we were living beyond our means in the Celtic Tiger, the three cars outside the door, all of that. You know how you'd notice? At Christmas someone might come in and say, "I'm having six people over for dinner, how many prawns do I want for prawn cocktails?" And I'd say thirty. They'd say, "no, give me a hundred". You'd know in your own heart and soul that seventy of those were going into the bin the following day, but it didn't matter, and "didn't matter" was the mentality that applied. There was an assumption that things would continue, but you had to be suspicious that a little island in the North Atlantic was showing the world the way in terms of growth.

'It was different in the 1970s and 1980s. Nobody was going to New York to buy their clothes for Christmas because it was cheaper to buy them there. In the 1980s, a taxi driver wasn't telling you that he had six properties that he owned around town, all of them rented out. There were extremes there that were surreal.

'When the crash came it was as though someone had thrown a switch, it was so sudden. People didn't realise the banks were in so much trouble in the crash, in particular. Every generation improved steadily in terms of its living standards but expectations seem to have risen to a level ... one thing that I notice from the counter is that a lot of the middle classes were hit in the last crash.

'In the 1980s it was a different shock, and more of the working classes were hit. And there was a shock compared to the crash, which you had to realise was inevitable. There was a hurt there because they were Cork businesses and they'd left so suddenly.'

The Market was hit with a second fire in January 1986: several stalls were destroyed and the roof was damaged, but the blaze did not cause the same level of damage as the earlier fire, thanks to the swift action of the Fire Brigade.

What is interesting about the Market's survival is the way it compresses many of the key elements of the wider story of Cork in the 1980s into one specific narrative. The comfortable routine shaken, and shocked, by decisions taken thousands of miles away; the defiance allied to innovation which helps an institution to survive; the intervention by key individuals – the female traders in this case – to make a difference; the interconnectedness of the Cork ecosystem; and the reliance on an inherent passion to get past initial obstacles.

Those specific elements would be seen again and again in the 1980s.

2

'Dickensian. Totally Hierarchical'

From the outside, Ford was one of the best jobs in Cork. Reliable, well-paid, prestigious: no wonder Red Crowley, who spent twenty years there, says it was like being in the bank. A permanent post in Ford – or Dunlop or Verolme – was a passport to the middle class for many. You could get a mortgage and move to wherever took your fancy in the city or beyond, for instance, an example of actual physical mobility as opposed to social climbing.

Behind the facade, however, there could be a different side to working in Ford. Much was always made of the long association between the American parent company and its Cork branch, the deep roots that Ford had in the community on Leeside.

The positive side to that was a deep loyalty that many workers – and customers – felt to the Ford brand, even in the aftermath of the closure.

But organisations which have habits and modes of practice dating back decades also run the risk of becoming sclerotic – to use the term applied in the 1980s to the Cork Film Festival, aptly enough. They can drift into hierarchical stasis and complacency, with disastrous results. It takes exceptionally clear vision to sift through the attractions of stability and comfort in order to identify the potential danger lurking just beneath the surface.

Dan Byrne studied electrical engineering in University College Cork (UCC) in the late 1960s and during his final year various firms and organisations came to the college on the 'milk round', signing up promising graduates.

'Many of the class went for interviews in the UK,' says Byrne. 'There was a big demand for graduates to work there, while others had interviews with the ESB, which at that time was an organisation run principally by engineers so they hired many Irish engineering graduates. I was offered a job in the ESB, which looked like a safe haven.'

Byrne and some members of his class had also been interviewed for a job in Ford, and though several of them were shortlisted, no jobs were offered. He decided to take the offer from the ESB and joined their offices in Dublin in September 1970.

'I wasn't there a month when I realised that it wasn't for me,' he says now. 'The toughest job I had was doing the crossword in the newspaper every day and I wasn't learning anything. At about that time I got a call from Fords to offer me a postgraduate position at their manufacturing plant in Cork.

'There was a culture of nepotism in Fords. If your father or uncle had a job there, you had every chance of being hired. At the interview I'd been asked if I had any relatives in Fords and I said no, but when I came home and told my parents how it went, including that question, my father said "What are you talking about – my brother's working there." My uncle Liam was

26

working there all his life but at the interview I'd totally forgotten it. I was thinking it hadn't gone that well anyway but I felt that put the tin hat on it altogether.'

Bored in the ESB, a long way from his native place, Byrne found the Ford offer an attractive proposition.

'It meant I could get back to Cork, so I was delighted when I was offered the position and joined in January 1971.'

Though he had excelled in UCC, Ford provided another level of education altogether for Byrne.

'I'd been in university for four years but I'd say I learned more in my first four months in Fords than I had in those four years in UCC. It was a huge learning experience for me. Interestingly, even though I had graduated as an electrical engineer, the work I was involved in at Fords was more mechanical, manufacturing and even civil engineering, rather than electrical engineering.

'The learning came through the plant director, Frank Dillon, who really ran Fords at that time. For some reason he took a special interest in my learning and afforded me the opportunity to be involved in all of the key activities in the plant. He exposed me early on in my career at a level I didn't deserve and which was way over my head – but I learned a huge amount from that, and I was very grateful to Frank and all of his management team for that experience. I worked there for four and a half years and I believe that I learned more in that time than I would have in another company in twenty years.'

Earmarked for progress, Byrne was given responsibilities that extended far beyond the factory floor, and as he puts it, his grounding in Ford prepared him for anything.

'When the Cortina TC was launched it was riddled with water leaks. You could not go into a car wash with it because you'd come out with the footwells full of water. The water just flowed into it.

27

'I remember Frank Dillon and the managing director, Paddy Hayes, asking me, as a young pup, to go and meet the governing body of the Ford dealers, twelve guys who represented all the Ford dealerships in the country. Now these were powerful, capable guys. Senior people. The likes of Tom Cavanagh in Fermoy, who owned his own company and was a huge influence personally on Ford Ireland itself, was one of those folks. I had to go to all of their premises to meet with the principals and promise that we were going to fix the water-leak problem.

'Now I was trying to justify the unjustifiable, really, but what a learning experience for me! Was I hammered by some of these guys? Absolutely, and with some justification on their part as their businesses were under threat due to the poor quality of the product. They weren't attacking me personally, they were attacking Fords. I was representing Fords, so I had to take it on the chin. It was a huge lesson and prepared me for other such experiences in the future.'

The advantage that Byrne had, however, was Ford's power in the Irish car market. The 1970s was a decade when the industrial powerhouses in the Far East hadn't quite woken up, and what was coming in from Japan did not impress many buyers.

'Ford had the lion's share of the car market, which wasn't surprising because there were very few Japanese cars, for instance. The Japanese were just entering the market at that time, and if the Cortina was leaky, some of the competitors' products were like sieves, in all honesty, with very poor quality. Much has changed since.'

While Byrne was at the main Ford plant in Cork's Marina, he noticed that life in the factory was heavily structured, with the symbolism of one's rank a frequent obsession.

'Fords was a very traditional company. Totally hierarchical and almost Dickensian. It was very status-conscious and everyone was very carefully graded. One joined at a certain grade – in my case a grade six – but to get to grade nine was the holy grail. That meant you were a manager with a company car, so everyone wanted to achieve this elusive goal.

'It was all about status and status symbols. As a manager you had your own private office, but it did not stop there. There were grade nines and grade nines – much also depended on your authority and power and influence and the symbols of that. The size and location of the office sent a message as did the fact of having some extra trappings, like a coat rack in the office, for example.'

Nothing summed up the caste system within the factory better than the eating arrangements.

'There were four canteens. There was a canteen for the men on the factory floor. There was a canteen for the office staff. There was a canteen for the grade nines, i.e., management. There was a canteen for the directors – the likes of Frank Dillon and Paddy Hayes. Each one of those canteens was used every day. Every single day there was a set lunch – catered by someone who was no Michelin star chef. The food was terrible. Genuinely. I would guess that the inmates in Mountjoy received better food.

'At one o'clock you went to the canteen, religiously, and you were back at your desk at one thirty. The bell went at one, you went to the canteen – workers, office staff, everybody. We all had our own tables and you ate with the same guys every day. I ate with many of the finance guys who worked across the road in Dunlop House, but who'd come across to the canteen every day at one.'

When the plant eventually closed, Paddy Hayes would become synonymous with the decision that put hundreds out of work. A decade earlier Byrne had found him sharp and focused, if distant.

'As MD, Paddy Hayes was a remote figure, a little aloof, really. He was more involved in sales and marketing than the running of the plant. I'd meet and interact with Frank Dillon every day, but I might see Paddy Hayes once a week. That was true for most people in the manufacturing environment, including the grade nines, who all reported in to Frank Dillon.

'Paddy Hayes was the role model when they hired me. He had studied civil engineering in UCC, was hired straight out of college and then put through the training programme that Ford had, which was pretty good. He came through all of that to eventually become MD of Ford Ireland.

'That was the path I was put on, too. That was the model. He had run the plant before becoming MD, and he certainly knew his stuff. I was at many meetings he chaired as MD and he was very decisive, a brilliant man in his own way. But Frank Dillon was my focus – all my learning came through him and his direct reports.'

Byrne was progressing in the company and was aware of the benefits of the job, as were his parents.

'My parents had worked very hard to put myself and my brother through university – my mother went out to work to earn money for that. They were delighted when I got a job in Cork, and in Fords … that was a job for life and had status. But after my first week in Fords my mother said to me, "why did we send you to university when you have to go to work at 8 a.m.?"

'The engineers started work at eight o'clock, when production started, while the finance staff in Dunlop House and the sales and marketing staff in the front office began work at 9 a.m. This was typical of the time. Office staff and management began work at 9 a.m. while production operatives began at the earlier time of 8 a.m. As part of the manufacturing unit we began work earlier with the rest of the production staff. My poor innocent mother's definition of failure was that I had to go to work at 8 a.m. rather than the later and more acceptable time of 9 a.m.'

After a few years, however, Byrne saw the pitfalls waiting down the road. The job was good and he was learning, developing his skills, but he could also see the danger of stagnation. When an opportunity came to get out of Ford, he took it – to general surprise.

'My decision to leave came when I was headhunted, though that term wasn't used then. A colleague I'd worked closely with in Fords went to work for AnCo [the employment and training body], which was a new organisation then. He was there around twelve months and kept ringing me to say it was great and I should join him there. We'd had a good working relationship in Fords and it was an attractive proposition, but my principal reason for leaving was looking at some of these famous grade nines, a lot of whom were twenty years older than me at that time.'

To the casual observer, these men had it made: senior management in the factory that underpinned a city's economic self-image. Corner offices and secretaries, status and money.

Byrne saw the reality up close, however: 'Some of them were broken men – either nervous wrecks or lacking self-confidence – and they were clearly unhappy with their lot. On the other hand they were very well paid so in some ways they were trapped. My view was simple – "when I'm forty or forty-five years of age do I really want to be like them? No way. I need to get out of here." That was totally a by-product of the culture in Fords rather than having anything to do with them as individuals. Some of these men were geniuses, some of the brightest people I ever worked with anywhere, and I'm not exaggerating.

'But the regime had broken them. It was totally dictatorial. I wasn't long in Fords when I was chatting to a colleague who was working in the industrial engineering office with me and I recall him saying to me, "Dan, you went to university for four years but that's no good to you here. The only training you need to survive here is to have spent six months living with the itinerants up in the Black Ash." He was speaking in jest but there was a huge amount of truth to that. It was dog eat dog there.'

Byrne decided to join AnCo, but his decision took some explaining, not least to his parents.

'When I decided to leave Fords, I went and told the two of them and they could not understand why I was leaving a permanent job and going to this other organisation. They didn't know anything about AnCo – I didn't know a lot more myself – but the idea that you would leave Fords was unheard of and therefore puzzled them.

'I told my manager I was leaving and I told Frank Dillon. There was some discussion to convince me otherwise – Frank pointed out how much I was learning and said I had a great future ahead of me in the company but my mind was made up. I said I appreciated it but I was going.'

Ford were decent to Byrne as he left, he recalls: 'Frank Dillon was a tough guy but a straight shooter, and he was very generous to me. When I got the offer from AnCo there had been a voluntary redundancy package available in Fords just a couple of months beforehand, as they were trying to reduce costs. By the time I got the offer that had expired, the time limit had passed. Frank said he'd look into that and, in fairness to him, he got me the package, so I got a lump sum that I'd never have been able to save.

'He didn't have to do that for me and it was probably against the rules of the scheme, technically, but he did it and I always appreciated it. So I was able to put that windfall towards the purchase of a house.'

His colleagues saw Byrne off with a going-away party at the Market Bar, but it wasn't long before the company reached out to him. Within nine months he got a phone call one Saturday morning from an old pal at the Marina.

'It was Joe Foley, one of the grade nines in Fords and one of those geniuses I referred to earlier. He rang to confirm we were playing golf that day, but the snow was thick on the ground the same morning. "If the balls are black, Joe, that's the only way we can play today," I said, but he insisted on coming out to collect me. I was living in Ballincollig and he said we'd head out to Macroom Golf Club anyway.'

Byrne found soon enough why Foley was so keen to hit the fairways: 'Frank Dillon had suggested to him that he ask me about coming back with the offer of a grade nine. That was the incentive. Joe was very convincing, and I knew he was speaking on behalf of Frank, but I said, "you know what you're telling me by offering me this – why didn't you give me a grade nine before I left? I might still be there." I might or might not have stayed, I'll never know the true answer to that but I told Joe that I was looking forward and that I was moving on. I wouldn't be going back. He was very understanding of my position and truthfully told me that he wished he had received such opportunities when he was my age.'

Byrne remembers his time in Ford with fondness: 'Despite some of the negatives, there was a great sense of camaraderie in Fords; it was like a close family and I made lifelong friends during my relatively short time there.' But he also recalls the reality of the period. Even a decade before the final curtain fell, Byrne saw danger on the horizon, and he had plenty of evidence for his pessimism.

'When I left Fords in 1975, I had a feeling in the back of my mind, "this thing cannot last". Much time and effort had been extended on the planning for a second and a third shift, which I had participated in.'

Extraordinary though it seems now, the Marina plant was working one shift instead of three, and was therefore idle much of the day.

'The demand was there for the product, and Cork was one of the few Ford plants in the world which didn't have three shifts, so we weren't fully sweating the asset, or maximising the return on capital. The factory was only in use eight hours a day, which was crazy. The unions were also involved in these discussions and they had their demands. People could certainly say the unions played a role in the failure of the second shift to take off because of their demands, but it would be unfair to say that. That would be too simplistic. There was more to it than that.'

Byrne is careful to point out that increasing the number of shifts would not necessarily have saved the factory.

'I'm not sure if the implementation of a second or a third shift would have made the Cork plant viable. I'm sure there are different opinions on that. However, my perception was there was also a lack of enthusiasm from management to embrace it as they saw it as a threat to their work life. If another shift were to be added, it would have meant extra work for all without any extra compensation. Many of these men had already given their lives to Fords and were close to retirement age, so they really had no incentive to promote such a strategy.

'Nobody was about to say out loud "no, we're not going to do that", but there was concern at a senior level about the second shift – a lack of enthusiasm in embracing it. If that enthusiasm had existed then the second shift would have happened, and any demands from the unions would not have stopped it. That's my opinion, based on my perception. It's not cast in concrete, and others might have different opinions, but that was my view.'

In time Byrne would put lessons learned in the Marina to work in another factory in Cork.

3

Dunlop: John McEnroe Says No

Niall Hartnett takes off his wristwatch and puts it down on the table.

'This is my father's watch. Dunlop's gave it to him after twenty-five years working there, and even that touch, giving employees a watch, was what set them apart. And it's a Gerard watch – he used to laugh about that because they were told Gerard were the Queen's jewellers, and there wasn't exactly a portrait of the Queen over the fireplace at home in our house. But that was the kind of gesture that made people loyal. And that's why there were people disappointed Dunlop's didn't step up with paying more in redundancy.'

Ford was the key employer in the Marina – and, at one stage, employed 7,000 workers, a number surpassed in Ireland only by the railways. Dunlop had deep roots in Cork as well, going back to 1934, when the factory began to produce tyres. From the start, however, it had been protected by legislation forbidding the importation of similar products except under licence, a harbinger of what would come fifty years later.

It soon diversified from pneumatic tyres into rubber footwear, rubber soles and heels, rubber hot water bottles, golf balls and tennis balls, and sundry other articles manufactured with rubber, and by the early 1960s its productivity was at an all-time high: 35,000 golf balls, 72,000 tennis balls and 1,500,000 pairs of shoes were being turned out annually by 2,500 employees in Cork, and the plant had to expand, spending £2 million in 1965 on a new office block in the Marina.

By then Dunlop wages were pumping £2 million per year into the local economy (at the time a pint of stout cost 11p) and it had acquired a Waterford rubber manufacturing company to aid in production. In the late 1960s worldwide demand for tyres (for cars and trucks) was growing at about 8 per cent per annum, and Europe, as one of the major growth areas, accounted for about one third of the world sales of car tyres and a quarter of truck tyre sales. Drumcora House, on the Old Blackrock Road, was bought by Dunlop jointly with its employees' social club, from the Egan family in 1972 for £20,000. Members paid 10d a week to the club to fund its purchase, rising over time to €5 a month, and it became the Dunlop Employees Social Club. Times were good, and only the best was good enough for the workers who were driving those good times.

Niall Hartnett's father, Christy, spent much of his working life in Dunlop, but not all of that time was spent on the factory floor, strictly speaking.

'My father went into Dunlop as a boy, as the term was, and at twenty-one he became a man there, a general operative working the three shifts. He got heavily involved in the then-

ITGWU [Irish Transport and General Workers Union] Number One Branch. It was associated with Dunlop's and textiles, and he got very involved in that and became a full-time shop steward in Dunlop's. At the time, it would have had over 2,000 people working there, so he had a full-time job. He wasn't necessarily making tyres but representing the workers.'

With over 2,000 employees to hand, Hartnett senior had a full day every day.

'There were six of us at home and when he'd come in after work we'd be all at him – "he's pulling my hair", "she's at me", the usual – and he'd say, "lads, I'm listening to people's problems all day long, can I have my dinner?" There's a different kind of trade union official now, but he was one of the old-style officials. There was another shop steward there, very popular, Jim Blake. He was on the national executive of the ITGWU; Gerry O'Sullivan, who later became a Labour TD, was another shop steward.'

In 1976 Christy Hartnett left Dunlop after working there for twenty-eight years and joined the ITGWU full-time: 'The No. 4 Branch to start with, but he ultimately ended up back with the No. 1 Branch in 1980 or so. So he became the union official representing people he'd worked with for twenty-eight years.'

It was a time when the bond forged at work didn't end at the factory gates. Niall Hartnett points to the summers that were shared by people who saw each other forty hours a week for the rest of the year as well.

'You're talking about people who worked together and who then, in the holidays, would have gone away together on holidays. The group my father was part of would have gone to Ballyheigue during the annual shutdown. It was in August – I think it later moved to July – when that happened, and the whole factory would go on holidays at the same time. We always went with the same group – the Cumminses from Fair Hill, the Finns, who were all involved with St Finbarr's. That would have been a regular thing, all in the same place together, and the other parents you'd call your aunts and uncles. It doesn't exist really any more, I suppose.'

It was on one of those holidays that Hartnett realised just how hard factory life could be.

'The best example was the time I met Mick Healy in Ballyheigue. Mick was from Blackpool – his father was Noel Healy who went on to play with Cork City – and on this particular day it was raining, but he was still heading in for a swim.

"You're going swimming in the lashing rain, Mr Healy," I said to him, and he said, "Niall, next week I'll be in the moulding shop." Meaning he was going to be sweating, the dirt of the mould, all of that, the work was dirty … at the time we were saying he was mad, but obviously he just wanted that last dip.

'They had great fun working there. The night shift was a horrible shift – my father used to say "even the cows in the fields sleep in the middle of the night" – but they had blackguarding to entertain each other. They worked hard but it was tough, working with rubber in the moulding shop would have been very hard.'

The factory had strong roots in the community.

'The Dunlop Sports and Social Club, that was a big thing – there was money there from the company for that, and there were other outlets. The Inter-Firm GAA leagues were very strong and Dunlop had a team in those, the same with the Shipping League in soccer. That was the social side outside of the work. Dunlop's was so big that it had interdepartmental sports tournaments. And that was a big part of why it was so central to people's lives.'

With the dawning of the 1980s there was a sense that the writing was on the wall, Hartnett says.

'It was always threatening. Joining the EU, or EEC as it was, in 1973, there'd been an embargo on foreign tyres coming in, and that was the writing on the wall. It was probably good at the time but clearly the tyre market was going to explode. That was certainly coming. And obviously it was cheaper to make tyres elsewhere. As we found out subsequently, that was true of almost everything.'

The Labour Court appointed John Horgan as a mediator between the unions and the company when the crisis eventually came, and the talks were conducted in the Harbour Commissioner offices. Hartnett's father was front and centre in the negotiations about redundancy packages.

'In our house they'd have been regarded as good employers. They paid well and paid regularly, and there was a loyalty to them: my parents wouldn't have spoken badly of Dunlop's, for instance But in my recollection Dunlop's didn't step up to the table when redundancies were forthcoming. They weren't as good as Ford's, for instance, and that was a disappointing. There were several votes taken during the negotiations, and between two of those votes my father collapsed. He was shifted to hospital by ambulance and I remember a fella out of Dunlop's standing across the road, watching what was going on. There was a photograph of him in the *Examiner* the following morning in his dressing-gown in hospital. That was the role he played.'

Hartnett can recall the politicians who called for briefings: 'The ones who would have been calling regularly would have been the likes of Senator Dino Cregan and Liam Burke, the TD. Dick Spring would have phoned the house regularly. My father was non-party, but they wanted updates, and I remember making tea and giving biscuits to Dino and Liam, say.

'A guy we would have been disappointed in around that time was Peter Barry, who was the senior minister in Cork, but he was away a lot of the time. He was Minister for Foreign Affairs, which meant he was away rather than being on the ground. The senators and TDs – Dino Cregan, Danny Wallace, Pearse Wyse, all of them were around.'

Another politician who took a keen interest in Dunlop was Toddy O'Sullivan, whose best friend worked in the factory.

'I remember reading a full-page advertisement in one of the English papers around that time which described how much Dunlop was going to invest in England. That angered me, and others. The Dunlop workers didn't come out that well. A lot of the jobs in Dunlop had a bonus attached, but their redundancy payment was based on their basic wage, which often was far lower than what they were getting week to week – and which they were used to, obviously.

'Added to that, the pension entitlements they were supposed to enjoy were delayed for a long time. There was a lot of dissatisfaction about that, naturally enough. It was terrible. I'd say it was the worst period in my political involvement. People were depressed and saw no hope.'

For Niall Hartnett the period remains raw in the memory: 'They all knew it was coming, but it's only when it's announced that it becomes real. The day the factory closed my father was at the gate and Tom McSweeney of RTÉ, Dick Hogan of *The Irish Times* and Val Dorgan from the *Examiner* were all there, and there was a photograph of the four them taken, surrounded by workers.

'For my father it was too close, too personal. He'd worked there for almost thirty years with all those people, he went on holidays with them, his life was wrapped up in the place. His brother Joe was playing hurling for Cork and down the Marina in the factory you had the Glen, the Barrs, Blackrock, all of that – and then he became lead negotiator when the plant was closing. They'd had strikes, they'd had arguments, but they were good employers. What hit home was that he knew a lot of his contemporaries – Jimmy Brohan, who played for Blackrock and

Cork, Georgie Murphy from the Glen, who was our next-door neighbour, all of those guys would struggle to find jobs.

'The closure was a done deal, and they were basically trying to get the best they could for the workers, but they also staged a sit-in. At the time Dunlop sponsored John McEnroe, the tennis player, and my father said if they gave a portion of what was being paid to McEnroe to the workers ...'

Eamon Young, a former All-Ireland-winning footballer and columnist in the *Evening Echo*, also beat that particular drum, and when McEnroe came to Ireland to play an exhibition match, he was met by some of the Dunlop workers, who put that proposition to him. As reported by *Sports Illustrated*, improbably enough, 'McEnroe expressed his sympathy for the workers' plight, but declined to make a contribution.'

Hartnett's father wasn't just disappointed by John McEnroe. 'I think he felt let down by the national executive of the ITGWU, that they weren't more supportive of the sit-in – that he felt very much left alone. When you think now of the Vita Cortex workers [when said workers agitated until they got their entitlements], their union was more supportive of them at a national level – maybe because the leader, Joe O'Flynn, was from Cork. But that's the only negative, that Dunlop's didn't pay more in redundancy. The workers may have gotten three weeks per year of service but Ford certainly paid more. Up to the closure they'd been very good employers, certainly, that was the only disappointment.

'It subsequently broke his health, that he didn't get what he wanted for them. He'd have been conscious that the Monday morning after it closed when all these people he knew and had worked with would be on the dole, he still had a job. Some of them never worked again. A few of them got jobs afterwards but not many and often not great jobs. My father retired early, in 1989, and without a doubt the closure had a huge effect on his health.'

As often happens in these circumstances, there was a brief flicker of hope. Toddy O'Sullivan can recall a briefing that Garret FitzGerald, then Taoiseach, gave Cork politicians, in which he said he had offered £8 million to Dunlop to stay, but the company had turned down the offer (FitzGerald also found time to write a letter of complaint to the *Examiner* about 'persistent misrepresentation' of his position on Dunlop, adding: 'your report that I "ruled out any idea of State intervention to save the firm" was accordingly the opposite of the true position'). Hartnett can remember rumours of a buyer.

'There was hope – there was talk at the time that a Chinese company or conglomerate was going to come in and replace Dunlop's, that it would start making tyres. There was a bit of hope about that, but really, apart from that there was nothing. There might even have been some kind of exploratory talks, but nothing came of it, either. I remember the machinery being packed up and shipped off. There are always a few people kept on for those jobs.'

In 1983, when the workers walked out of the gates, however, it was all over, and 850 people were out of work.

'My memory was that the banks were all represented down there the day it closed, because fellas were getting tidy money – three weeks' wages per year if you worked there twenty or thirty years or more was obviously a fair amount. Some of them managed it badly, obviously. That was inevitable. Most of them were middle-aged with kids and that was the focus.

'I still see lads who worked with my Dad. Pa Finn lives next door to me, and we went on holidays with them. My Dad left Dunlop's in 1976 and so did Pa – he became a rep and he found it hard in terms of being lonely after working with hundreds of people.'

Hartnett adds that his family were in an odd position after the closure: 'We had good times out of Dunlop's. We didn't feel the pain that other families felt, and that's hard to say. We didn't feel that financially because my father still had a job. If he'd stayed in Dunlop's he would have lost his job at fifty-three, fifty-four – who'd have given him a job at that stage? They were general operatives who couldn't go anywhere else at that stage. Val Dorgan was a good support to my father, it was a two-way thing. While there was no social media or anything, the coverage was still huge. There was talk at one stage of flying my father to Dublin for *Seven Days* or *Today Tonight*, whichever was the current affairs programme at the time. Nothing came of that, but that kind of focus, combined with the stress of representing fellas he knew so well for so long, it took a toll.'

It was a potent reminder of Cork's place in the world, Hartnett feels.

'For us in Cork, Dunlop's was big, but for the company itself it was small stuff. And for the company it was probably the right decision. For a thousand people and their families in Cork it was a terrible decision, but for Dunlop's, they had to make tyres as cheap as they could. You'd have been shot if you said that, and we'd have been conscious that someone could have said, "easy for you to say that, your father still has a job." We'd have been very conscious of that.'

Toddy O'Sullivan points out that the closure of the factory did not end the effect on some employees of the work they had done there.

'The workers had had a good standard of living and a lot of them had committed themselves to building their own houses, they were putting kids through college – Ford workers seemed to come out better in the settlement received because their payment structure was different. I thought it was back-door methods from Dunlop, bearing in mind that it could be a dangerous job. They were dealing with chemicals which would affect one's health.

'For years afterwards, former members of Dunlop staff would come to Connolly Hall to be examined by a doctor, specifically regarding the effects of those chemicals. This was obviously a time long before health and safety regulations featured.'

Niall Hartnett's father also found the factory cast a long shadow.

'He was regularly called to the courts afterwards as a character witness on behalf of the odd former Dunlop worker who had gotten into trouble later, after the redundancy money had run out.

'Some of the lads who got money thought it would last forever, obviously, and when it didn't some of them got into trouble. My father would regularly testify in court that the closure of the factory had had a devastating effect on the person's health and so on, so it lasted for years after as well. He'd come in and say "I was in court today, so-and-so was up." So it happened. It kept carrying on.'

4

Verolme: Selling the Job Twice

Shipbuilding had been an industry in Rushbrooke, near Cobh, for a couple of centuries before the main shipyard was taken over in 1958 by Verolme Dockyards of Holland, thanks largely to the efforts of Seamus Fitzgerald, J.P. Beddy of the IDA and Brian Gallagher, the Irish Ambassador to the Hague.

The Dutch influence in the dockyard was significant. They brought a serious work ethic and drive to the Cobh area, and the prospect of working with the very latest in technology attracted people like Joe Tuohy of Tipperary. Tuohy's first job had been in the sugar company in Mallow ('A strange place to work – you worked flat out for twenty-four hours a day, seven days a week, during the sugar season, but then the whole thing stopped and the factory was torn apart and rebuilt.')

An engineer, Tuohy was taken on in the sugar factory, along with some science graduates, and put to work with the shift supervisors: 'They knew everything about the place. One of them was Dick Harnedy, the great Cork footballer of the 1940s – and though the place was highly unionised, there was an incredible work ethic there. Very constructive. In the off-season everything, almost, in the factory would be rebuilt, and I was put in charge of the workshops, to rebuild the vessels, the tanks, the pipework, and that got me interested in welding.

'We got more responsibilities over the coming years – and learned more about people, maybe, than the sugar industry – but when Verolme advertised for people to work in non-shipbuilding activities I applied, went for interview and got switched on, really, by the place. It was a big operation, workshops, the shipyard – cutting edge for the time, certainly. The Dutch lads there had a form of desktop computer as early as 1965, for instance.'

Significantly enough, Verolme even then was diversifying. Though synonymous with shipbuilding and ship repair, the dockyard was already looking at other avenues, other income streams, and Tuohy became part of that.

'We were doing fenders for the Port Talbot terminal, walkways for the terminal down in Whiddy Island, the Valentia bridge was built in the dockyard and floated down there, the big fermenters for Pfizer were built there.

'The dockyard had a lot of skills built up in shipbuilding and repair. A German company was building a nitric acid plant for a project and we bid for the construction of it. I remember being sent off to Germany to discuss it and ringing home from Dortmund for permission to sign off on the contract. Mr Vanderpoul was at the bottom of a ship in Cobh and had to come up out of it to take the call and say yes. We sent thirty or forty fellas up to do the job.

'A French company came in to build the power plant in Campile on Great Island in Wexford and again, we sent forty or fifty fellas down to work on that, too. They stayed in digs down there and for three years we rented a train to bring them in and out there – every day for three years. There was a great foreman on the job, Joe Stack, and Matt O'Mahony was the engineer on the job. It worked out very well. That was all separate from the shipbuilding itself.'

Tuohy saw other areas for Verolme to expand into as the 1970s dawned. Given the negativity about European tariffs that arose in the mid 1980s when factories were closing in Cork, it is noteworthy to see the interest continental companies were beginning to take in Ireland.

'Two more things had an impact. The Irish power plant market was interesting – every company in Europe wanted to get into it. The units were smallish compared to those in Europe, the latest ones, but it was a market they were all able to compete in as part of their standard manufacturing, so those big companies all competed strongly.

'One of them, Braun Bavaria, was probably the top technical company in the world at that time and we agreed to manufacture stuff under licence for them. They'd gotten a lot of power station work already. Also, when there weren't power stations up for bidding they started to give us subcontracting work.

'That worked fine and was profitable enough but they gave us one very difficult job – difficult technically. That was manufacturing sealing rings for high pressure: these were circular, heavy, made from special metals, and the precision involved was very tight even by today's standards. The dockyard put the man in charge of the workshops over that, as a full-time supervisory job in quality control. The sealing rings were going into one of the biggest turbines in the world at that time – a power station in the US, I think.

'After they were delivered I followed them out to Baden to meet Mr Edelman from Braun Bavaria. With a little trepidation. I went in to meet him and he stood up and said, "What wonderful quality from Ireland." It made my day.'

The approval of Braun Bavaria was significant, says Tuohy, as it gave more confidence to the workforce, skilled as it was: 'That's a measure of what the dockyard could do – the measure of the people and the skills that were there. The furniture for the ships was all made there in a separate workshop. Wonderful stuff.'

Tuohy himself decided to spread his wings, but when he did Verolme also benefited: 'I applied for a Fulbright scholarship without telling the boss – those scholarships were open to people in industry and business, then, though academics have it captured now. I got it and told the boss, and he agreed – my wife agreed too, which was very accommodating, given we had two kids. She said to go for it.

'I went to Berkeley – and got rid of any inferiority complex about Irish education while I was there. I felt at undergraduate level we'd outpace them, though at postgraduate they'd leave us for dead. I made a lot of friends and learned a lot, but the last part allowed me to travel around the US for a month. The last American consul in Cork, John Beeds, took a paternal interest in people going to the States if they didn't let him down, and I'd given him a list of places I'd like to see. I got to see some big engineering companies and visited NASA. I was in the Washington Press Club when the Apollo 9 astronauts came in, all of that.'

While in Houston, Tuohy dropped in on an organisation with a dubious enough reputation now, thanks to its former CEO Dick Cheney, but which was a force in heavy engineering and manufacturing even then.

'While I was there I went to see Brown and Root – Haliburton now – who were building these massive modules for the Alaskan oilfields. They were huge units, loading them on barges and shipping them off. I was thinking "we could do that in Ireland, the North Sea is opening up."'

When he got back to Verolme, Tuohy told his boss about the offshore work Brown and Root were doing ('so he felt the trip hadn't been a waste of time') and got clearance to look into it, to see if there was a potential growth area for the dockyard.

'There was a big offshore conference in Aberdeen, and Fergus Cahill of the IIRS [Institute for Industrial Research and Standards] had been given the job of ensuring there was Irish content in the offshore Marathon project at Kinsale.

'Fergus had no budget for going to Aberdeen and my boss – a far-seeing Dutchman, Mr Vanderpoul, one of the most brilliant men I ever met, could talk quantum physics, relativity, anything – said "why don't we pay for Fergus and you can go with him?"

'I went chasing around the oil companies in London for a couple of years – Phillips, Shell, Esso – getting to know people personally and getting them interested, and the big breakthrough came with Phillips. They had a huge number of big fields in the North Sea, they were one of the early developers, and the head man agreed to come to Cork to see the dockyard and see if they could give us some of the work. He arrived, but there was no ship in construction he could see.'

It was a disaster. They'd done the hard job, getting the Phillips boss to travel all the way to Cork, but an empty yard was no help. Then Vanderpoul had a brainwave.

'We'd recently built the LE *Eithne*, so Vanderpoul contacted the Naval Service. Liam Brett was commanding the LE *Eithne* and heading out past Roche's Point, but they got in touch with him, he turned back in, the man from Phillips went on board the ship and satisfied himself that all the skills had been used to construct the ship. And we got a contract building for them as a result.

'That led to work from Shell and Marathon later. We did work for the ESB and one of the senior ESB guys contacted me about an Irish company which was starting up to work on power stations, a subsidiary of General Electric. The company was Atlantic Plant and I was offered a job as construction engineer in Tarbert. I'd bid for that job from the dockyard, as it happens, but it doubled my salary so we went off to Tralee for a couple of years, and I left the dockyard.'

Much like Ford, Verolme was a place of hierarchies. Tuohy remembers that his line manager was someone he knew very well – but not quite well enough to be on first-name terms.

'In Verolme there was a canteen for the management, another canteen for the workers … the Dutch mightn't have been as hierarchical as the Germans, but they still emphasised it. It was always "Mr Vanderpoul", and though I knew him well I never called him by his first name, Gerard.'

Tuohy describes the Dutch company as 'straight and fair', adding that in the 1960s and 1970s there would have been plenty of them with vivid memories of the Second World War: 'To them, Ireland was a revelation. They got into riding horses and messing around in boats, and the sheer room they had here compared to Holland, they really enjoyed it.'

The social side was strong in the dockyard, and the Dutch would have pushed that, adds Tuohy: 'Every year there was a dinner dance in the Metropole and all the management were obliged to go to that, the Dutch management were very strong on that. I founded the golf society, we had a hurling team, there was a soccer team. It was strong in those terms, the things that help create that atmosphere.'

The work ethic was every bit as strong as was rumoured, however. There was an urban legend that a worker was once killed in an on-site accident in Verolme and as his colleagues left the yard in shock immediately afterwards, they could see the Dutch continuing to work.

'There was a great saying in the dockyard if something difficult or challenging came up,' says Tuohy, 'Someone would say, "you'd want to be years at it – or six months in Holland." That encapsulated the Irish view of the Dutch.'

At the Irish end, Tuohy says management was good: 'Sean Reilly of Cobh was a shop steward in Verolme – his son is now Archbishop of Cashel and Emly – and he was a dynamo of a shop steward, very personable, and he and the managing director effectively ran the dockyard. Finbarr Ronayne became chairman after a couple more old-fashioned chairmen, and Finbarr and Vanderpoul ran the business end of the dockyard, basically, out of the Silver Springs Hotel.

'Finbarr was only thirty-eight when he was appointed but he was a great choice. They were crucial, those three guys. You might wonder what difference three people could make in a place which had 1,400 working in it when I left, but they did. The problem, though, was that shipbuilding had become an artificial industry worldwide.'

Tuohy points out that some of Ireland's shipbuilding disadvantages could not be helped, like geography. The economics of the world market did not help, and the internal organisation of the company did not favour Cobh, either – the Dutch were always going to favour their home base over a far-flung outpost in the final analysis.

'Ireland fell behind the likes of South Korea and Japan once they turned to serious shipbuilding. Ireland was always going to be at the bottom of the food chain in that regard. If push came to shove, the Dutch were always going to walk away from Cobh before they'd walk away from Rotterdam, obviously. That was why Vanderpoul always wanted to diversify, they could see that coming.

'There were three legs to the stool in the dockyard, really. Ship repair was steady enough work, though probably not that profitable. The saying about it was that you had to sell the job twice – once to get the ship into the dockyard, and then, when the work was done and you assessed what it cost, you had to then sell the invoice. It was very unusual. They were good at that, but it was limited because of the size of the dry dock.

'Then you had shipbuilding itself, which was cyclical, but they maintained a steady enough stream of work allocated by the head office in Holland; they had seven or eight shipyards in the group.

'And then you had the other projects we worked on, the engineering and so on, which was part of the move to diversification. To this day the dockyard is a great facility, and there's a lot of small businesses doing well down there.'

By 1983 the writing was on the wall for Verolme, and the government knew it, having accepted a report from a consultant who had examined the dockyard's commercial prospects. His conclusion was stark and simple: the dockyard was not viable.

At the time almost 1,100 staff were employed in the dockyard, but the consultant's view was that it had no prospect of securing either foreign or domestic orders due to its low productivity rates and high prices.

The company had been profitable up to 1978, but it felt the squeeze in what would later be described as the worst slump in living memory in the global shipbuilding industry, which took effect from the mid to late 1970s onwards.

Cabinet records released under the thirty-year rule revealed that, at a cabinet meeting in May 1983, John Bruton, then the Minister for Industry and Energy, recommended that the government not place any more orders with Verolme for patrol or fisheries vessels. Bruton pointed out that both B&I and Irish Shipping had no requirement for new vessels. Clearly, this was bad news, particularly in light of the fact that Verolme had submitted a survival plan, but that plan depended on two orders for vessels needed by the state. Those orders would delay the need to secure foreign orders until early 1984.

Unfortunately, the lack of competitiveness then hit Verolme: while the Department of Fisheries and Forestry did want to order a new research vessel, Verolme's original quote had risen from £3 million to £7 million, compared to a rival quote by a Norwegian shipbuilder, which came in at £4 million. A cabinet memo from the time claimed that foreign orders could only be obtained with massive government subsidies because the dockyard was uncompetitive; not just uncompetitive, in fact: subsidies to the extent of up to 100 per cent of order prices were needed.

'Even if the government were prepared to meet the prohibitive costs of such subsidies, there is no possibility that such aid levels would be permitted by the European Commission,' the memo added, going on to state that there was no compelling argument for keeping Verolme open either to save jobs or for strategic reasons.

Bruton laid more unpalatable truths on the table at the meeting: he pointed out that the last time Verolme had won a foreign order was in 1975, at the height of the shipbuilding boom but even that success had only come through its Dutch parent company. He pointed out that the majority Dutch shareholder had also left the Rushbrooke facility to its own devices in terms of sales, marketing, and technical assistance for many years.

The government of the time supported the provision of 'delivery incentives' to ensure the timely completion of vessels which it had already ordered in 1980 to assist the shipyard during a crisis caused by a lack of orders. Even then it had not been competitive – the orders included a new bulk carrier for Irish Shipping, despite the fact that it cost £29 million, which was twice as much as the price quoted by rival bidders at the time.

Alan Dukes, the Minister for Finance, said the consultant's report showed Verolme's survival had been solely due to the provision of state orders for ships which were 'seriously overpriced and in some cases unnecessary'. Dukes opposed ordering a new fisheries vessel, as he said it would amount to 'a major waste of public funds'.

Liam Kavanagh, the Minister for Labour, expressed concern that the disclosure of the plans for Verolme's fate would be managed in a sensitive manner in order to minimise the ill feeling that already existed among staff towards the company because of the lack of information about the shipyard's future; Kavanagh urged the cabinet to apprise trade union representatives at Verolme of the situation as quickly as possible and advised his ministerial colleagues that 'a very militant stance' could be expected by Verolme staff on the question of redundancy.

Foreign Minister Peter Barry – a Cork native – opposed Bruton's recommendations, claiming the difficulties faced by Verolme were 'by no means unique' and other countries like the Netherlands and Sweden had provided huge subsidies to their shipbuilding industries. He criticised the consultant's report for failing to examine in detail its preferred option – for Verolme to move to a 50 per cent reliance on ship repair and to concentrate future shipbuilding on offshore supply vessels for which there was a good demand.

Barry argued such a measure would maintain 75 per cent of the jobs at Rushbrooke, but Bruton reminded him that the 'preferred option' was dependent on the unlikely scenario of Verolme winning new foreign orders.

'Unlikely' was a euphemism. Verolme closed in November 1984 and 500 jobs were lost.

5

The Fall Guy: Paddy Hayes

In a city the size of Cork, the head of one of the biggest employers in the area was bound to be a well-known individual. Thus Paddy Hayes, the managing director of Ford, was a prominent figure in the life of the city.

Hayes was a local boy, educated at the North Monastery, and had risen through the ranks to head Ford affairs in the country, but he was a distant figure.

'Aloof,' is journalist Donal Musgrave's description. 'I had good contacts at union level, and they were tipping me off that things weren't going well long before the closure was announced. That's why we set up an interview with Paddy Hayes.

'I went down to the factory to meet him and was made to wait, the usual stuff. The office was nice – he was chauffeur-driven everywhere he went, loved opera, and let that be known to people.

'I wasn't a fan of his. I found it very hard to get information from him. It was certainly like getting blood from a stone that day, and as a result I don't have any strong memories of the interview. That rankled, and it came down through the management. I remember going to a critical meeting of union and management in the old Jury's Hotel one time and I had a hand put up to my face to stop me from coming in. The management were all-powerful.'

In time the release of cabinet documents would endorse Musgrave's view. Hayes had been in contact with successive governments to brief them on the plans for the Marina and much of the correspondence was the cliché one might expect: compliments to the politicians, cautious optimism about the future.

Hayes had written to Taoiseach Charles Haughey in 1982, for instance, warning that the future of the Cork plant was reliant on the successor to the venerable Cortina saloon, which had been one of the best-selling cars in Europe for years.

'We attach great importance to the assembly of the new [Ford] Sierra because the future of Ford Ireland and its 1,100 employees depends to a great degree on its sales success both in Ireland and in Europe generally,' Hayes wrote, adding an invitation to Haughey to visit the plant. (This was a significant change in the weather from the previous year, when Hayes had written to then-Taoiseach Garret FitzGerald, outlining Ford's policy and complimenting FitzGerald on 'the guts and the integrity to do all the right things since your election … I did it [the briefing] together with Mr Ford himself with Liam Cosgrave. Peculiarly, however, your predecessor [Haughey] refused to see me.')

In another letter to the government – dated 23 January 1984 – Hayes said he was saddened by the closure announced on 17 January that year: 'I am sure that you [Garret FitzGerald] will understand that, apart from the 800 people losing their jobs, my personal regret and sadness is more intense that any other Irishman's could be.'

The key revelation in those cabinet papers was a handwritten note, however, from an anonymous civil servant saying Hayes 'talks to G. Almighty only.'

In comparison to others in similar roles, Hayes was far better known. His equivalent in Dunlop, for instance, had a far lower profile.

'Joe Davis would have been on the opposite side to the union in those negotiations,' says Niall Hartnett. 'He was one of the major figures. My father would have been known for one or two things, but one thing he used to say was, "with a multinational you're only a phone call away from being closed down". And that was repeated elsewhere later.

'But in terms of those discussions, they never became personalised. Joe Davis wasn't putting himself out there maybe to the extent that Paddy Hayes did – people didn't know who he was to the same extent. My father might have mentioned Joe in passing, so we knew who he was, but he wasn't a public figure, certainly.'

Because Hayes was seen as remote – and had, after all, delivered the news to hundreds of people that their jobs had gone – there was a tendency at the time to conflate him with the decision to shut the plant down. To personalise matters, as Hartnett says. But as he also points out in relation to the closure of Dunlop: 'Those decisions hadn't been made in the Marina. They were made in Dunlop's head office.'

The same could be said of Ford, and in the car assembly industry, there were even more factors at play. The time bomb for the car industry had been ticking away in the background for years. It took the form of the restriction on car imports which had been agreed when Ireland joined the European Economic Community (EEC) in 1973. The negotiations were difficult but Irish Minister for External Affairs Dr Patrick Hillery won the day with the concession.

And at the time it was seen as a win. A government paper on the car industry in Ireland outlined the rationale behind the deal: 'As part of the arrangements for the transitional period of EEC membership, a special 12-year protocol was negotiated for the motor industry. This grew out of the recognition that motor assembly on the small scale prevalent in Ireland was unlikely to be viable in full free trade conditions ...'

Because of this concession, the car-assembly industry in the country was getting over a decade to diversify and become more competitive, with plenty of advance notice of the exact date on which Ireland would become an open market: 1 January 1985.

Throughout the 1970s, other issues arose to make those efforts to diversify trickier, however. In the same year that Ireland joined the EEC there was a petrol crisis, and the after-effects from that crisis would continue to be felt throughout the decade. It was seen correctly as the harbinger of a global downturn, with increasing costs in every sector linked to the price of oil.

In Ireland itself, within four years of joining the EEC the number of companies involved in assembling motor vehicles went from twenty-two in 1962 to fourteen, another ominous sign.

The whole area of car assembly also changed. With the oil crisis and the global economic recession, there was a greater awareness of the need for fuel efficiency, which in turn led manufacturers to focus on smaller, more efficient cars. Among the imports that would flood into the country from 1 January 1985 were Asian cars which fitted that bill perfectly.

The pieces of the jigsaw were slowly sliding into place, but in Cork there was optimism even then. For instance, when Henry Ford II himself visited the Marina for the company's sixtieth anniversary in June 1977, he hinted that, rather than contract, there were plans to create a further 800 jobs in Cork: 'Certainly, we look at Ford of Ireland as a vital link in the Ford of Europe sales and manufacturing chain. That is why I see no reason for any reduction in the Cork plant's importance. The almost 20,000 new Ford vehicles we are building in Ireland this year create a continuing demand for Irish-made paints, glass, tyres and tubes, upholstery materials, batteries, lamp bulbs, and spark plugs that go into their assembly.'

Contrary to Ford's optimism, the coming years were tough. The Cork plant had been traditionally aligned with the Ford works in Dagenham, where many Corkonians had found employment in the past. When it was announced that that foundry was closing and 2,000 jobs were going, the signs were even worse for the Marina plant. Then Dunlop closed.

'There had been that sense early in the 1980s that Ford was going to build an engine factory,' says Red Crowley, 'And there was talk that that would be built in Cork. It ended up somewhere else, not Cork, and soon after that Dunlop closed.

'When that happened people were saying it was a matter of time. I think fellas' heads were dropping from around 1982 on – losing out on the engine factory was a blow, because that would have meant increasing the workforce. After Dunlop's it was more a case of "how long can we last?"'

Comparisons were being made between Ford in Cork, producing approximately 400 cars a week, and the Belgian plant, which was producing almost 6,000 per week. The disinclination to open second and third shifts, as evidenced by the reaction to

Dan Byrne's research the previous decade, now began to bite. Cork was nowhere near as productive as it might have been, clearly.

The lethal combination of international factors and local challenges meant the Marina plant was vulnerable and ultimately doomed. Hayes was just the one who delivered the bad news.

6

Lacking Context: Coverage of the Closures

The way the closures were covered fed into the general despair also. What would now be termed media platforms were few and far between in the 1980s – RTÉ radio and television, the *Evening Echo* and the *Cork Examiner* – and of those outlets the last-named dominated the local news agenda.

And of those outlets, while the *Examiner* dominated the coverage of the closures, one man dominated the tone of that coverage. Val Dorgan had been the newspaper's hurling writer, and a very good one, wryly characterising the ideal holder of that post as an All-Star himself for the sake of credibility – but representing Mars in order to establish his impartiality.

From the GAA beat, Dorgan went to cover European affairs. If it was a marked departure from his previous beat, again,

Dorgan pointed out years later that, in comparison with the emotions generated by the local hurling championship, nobody had ever wanted to punch him in a Cork chipper because of what he was writing about fish quotas. By the mid 1980s he was a long-standing columnist with a powerful platform that was required reading on Leeside.

In the newsroom he was a strong personality. One new journalist could recall, years after the event, being shown to a vacant desk on his first day in the *Examiner* in the 1980s. He soon became aware of a looming, silent presence behind him: Dorgan. The new man had been shown to his seat as a joke, but he got up immediately and let the senior man sit down.

When it came to covering Ford and Dunlop in particular, Dorgan was dealing with subjects and people he knew well. As a hurler with Glen Rovers in the early 1950s, he had played with men who worked in the two factories, and in covering the local championship in the Athletic Grounds he would have travelled past Ford and Dunlop on countless Sundays, often writing about men who would return to work there on Monday. When he won an All-Ireland minor hurling medal in 1951, the star on the Cork team had been his club mate Johnny Clifford, who would put down years in Dunlop. The links went on and on.

Because of those connections the tenor of the media reaction was one of simple betrayal, says Pat Casey, a staff reporter of the time.

Asked if there was any reporter seeking to widen the economic context or to offer an international perspective on what was happening down the Marina, Casey says to have raised such issues in editorial conferences in Academy Street would have had one immediate challenge.

'First he'd have had to duck from Val Dorgan, but you're right. The enormity of the impact registered only after a few days. It was a betrayal. A betrayal of Cork, a betrayal of those who had given Ford's their working lives – they had been thrown on the scrapheap. That was the phrase, and for once it's not a bad description. The chances of those made redundant finding another job were very slim, particularly when the cascading effects of the other closures came on stream.'

The connections between Dorgan and his old teammates was replicated across the newspaper, he adds.

'In the *Examiner* of the time, your merit was judged by your level of indignation about the closures, and we all bought into it. We all knew people who were working there, and it was our first real exposure to the ruthlessness of corporate decision-making. They were all bastards and we were the victims: there was no analysis, really, and it was piled one on top of each other. The stories were of devastation and hurt, which were all valid, but looking back now, from a journalistic point of view it was limited enough.

'Nowadays, though you might think plants on that scale don't really exist any more, Apple and the pharma companies have a huge presence in Cork. When one closes you have that twenty-four to forty-eight hours of people coming out of factories saying "we're devastated, we don't know what we're going to do now", and then the analysis kicks in – analysis of the business case, why the place has closed, and it becomes much less emotive.

'But that wasn't the case in Cork then. And part of that is the significance of the *Examiner* at the time. It was the bible. Part of the fabric of Cork. It didn't really have any competition at the time in Cork, not from the *Times*, the *Press* or the *Independent*. They didn't go much beyond a similar reaction though there was a bit more in the business pages, maybe.

'There was a sense that Cork had taken an undeserved hit – that everything Ford had said about what Cork represented had been forgotten about. To a degree, it was a seminal period for Cork, becoming victims for everything. I know there might be people outside of Cork who'd say Cork are very good at that, but this was certainly the high-water mark for it.'

Casey in time pointed out that the *Examiner* needed to move to the next stage, to work out what was next for the city, but the tastes of the time inclined to blaming people rather than sober scrutiny.

'I remember writing a column at one point where I said I felt the *Examiner*'s editorial disposition at the time actually inhibited the kind of reflection and analysis that was required on where Cork was going next. We spent a lot of time blaming Ford's and Dunlop's and not enough time saying "this is the real world now, what do we do next?"

'People were flailing. There was a lot of heat and not a lot of light, put it that way. Of course, the blame game started and because the analysis was so simplistic – there was no analysis, really – then politicians got a kicking for not producing a solution. "Why didn't ye stop it, why didn't ye give them what they were looking for", that sort of thing. But Ford, for instance, were looking for something that Cork couldn't give: a scale of operation for assembly and manufacturing that would have had to increase tenfold.'

Looking back now, over thirty years later, were people living in denial? When Casey describes people as being shocked by the closures while still expecting them, it seems a reasonable way of illustrating how many felt at the time, holding out unrealistic hopes in the face of the inevitable.

'There was a sense that "they couldn't do that to us, really", that there was a Corkman in charge ... silly defence mechanisms were being put up, but it was well flagged. There were rationalisations going on in the automotive industry all over Europe, and anybody with a sense of the scale of the operation in Cork compared to other operations in Europe, they must have known.

'That said, I remember reading a piece which described staff at the time as expecting it but still being shocked, if that's not a contradiction. There was a palpable shock when it did arrive, even though people were fearing it.'

Though social media was far in the future, there was a good deal of talk ahead of the announcements themselves, not least when the dominos started to fall in earnest. The technology might have been primitive, but that did not stop discussion.

'The mechanisms were limited. The *Examiner*, the *Echo*, RTÉ and that was about it. I think people networked better then and spoke more, so there was an undercurrent of information which compensated for deficits in communication.

'I don't think there was a lack of information. If you have 800 people and there's discussion there, that multiplies outside. In journalism circles there wasn't shock – there had been meetings, political fears expressed, all the normal prelude to something like that.

'I think that must have had an effect, I knew a lot of the lads from Dunlop's – and Ford's – from coming into the family pub, and there was a sense of gathering momentum, that the era of big manufacturing plants in Cork would become a thing of the past – or that decisions would be made in favour of bigger units. People understood that, some less well than others, and I always thought Ford's was more highly regarded in Cork as a job. It had a particular status, the Henry Ford connection, all of that conveyed something – and even that connection became a straw people grasped at.

'Dunlop's was a tougher, dirtier job which didn't have a pristine, striking end product you could say, "God, look at that, it was made in Cork", so Ford's was seen as the premier posting:

it was seen as tantamount to having a farm of land. You had a job for life there, the conditions were good, you were well paid, parents' attitude generally would have been "stay there, you're lucky" – so the rug was pulled out from all of that when it went.'

Working back from that, the sense of having made it if you landed into one of those jobs, the depression as a consequence of losing that job, explains the sense of betrayal in the media coverage. Not only were the jobs gone, the most basic support structures for hundreds of people suddenly put on the dole were lacking.

'It was flagged, but the closure was catastrophic, really. There were 800 people working there and the multiples of other jobs being sustained by those were probably two per manufacturing position – that meant 2,400 jobs. Add in Dunlop's and Verolme and you're talking about multipliers at the extreme end of economic crisis.

'Training and preparing people for change was virtually non-existent. That's better handled now, and the units involved are also smaller, so you don't have the numerical impact that Ford's and Dunlop's had, but it was the worst possible time in that there was no training infrastructure, very little support of any sort.

'Why wasn't there a Vita Cortex situation? That may have related to the conditions under which Ford's departed. I didn't get the sense at the time that people were dissatisfied with those conditions. I don't think there was an undercurrent of militancy leading people to occupy buildings and so forth.'

Casey argues that the sense of inevitability about the closures combined with what was then an innate conservatism.

'People had their "place", even though that's very much in inverted commas. The leadership would have been conservative as well, don't forget. There wouldn't have been people coming from left field to suggest other options. Looking at the closure of the sugar beet factory in Mallow in comparision, there would have been a lot of on-street activity when that occurred. But that was twenty-odd years after this period. It was clearly a different time in 2006, to 1984 or 1985. Back in the mid 1980s expectations were different. It was a traditional industry, and traditions were important. There was a way of doing things and people didn't rock the boat.

'Plus, there was another sense, one of "what difference would it make, anyway?" People were fatalistic. It wasn't as if someone had just decided to fly in and the place was gone twenty-four hours later. There were concerns for a number of years, obviously, and now they'd come home to roost.'

7

The Fallout: 'I Used to be Someone'

Evidence of the closures filtered out in odd ways once the initial shock passed. Pat Casey can remember trace elements even as he drove into the city every morning.

'Coming in to work from Carrignavar direction through to the city, for months I was passing groups of men out walking. Some with dogs, some without, some chatting to each other, some not. Before that you'd pass the odd man out walking, but now there were groups. Four or five at a time coming up Dublin Hill or out the Commons Road, out further towards Glenville and coming all the way around again. It was noticeable, the number of people out walking. They were all unemployed. What else were they doing?'

It's an arresting image: middle-aged men converted more or less overnight to the virtues of long country strolls in order to kill time. Former Minister of State Kathleen Lynch can remember that the interconnectedness of the communities, the fact that so many people got relatives and friends to work in the factories, led to entire streets becoming jobless overnight.

'The other side of it is that Ford's, Dunlop's, Verolme, those were very good places to work. The unions were strong, the money was good, and the difference nowadays is that unionisation is coming back slightly, while during the boom people felt they didn't have a need for a union. But in the 1980s it was all the more catastrophic for having happened overnight, almost. It was a bit like the IMF, it wasn't going to happen and then, suddenly, it happened.

'People I knew in Dunlop at the time, who were very clued in, would have had suspicions. There were people coming in and out for meetings, talks going on, company management going to head office, so they might have been a little more prepared, but for most people it was a bolt out of the blue. Waterford Glass was similar, as was Dell in Limerick. And this was where the family links, and the whole system of neighbours getting each other into those places had another effect. Whole streets became unemployed because the son next door and the guy two doors down were all pulled in – and now it was gone.'

People's reactions were not always as predictable as one might have expected either. Ford and Dunlop had been good places to work and there was every chance you got to hear exactly how good they were, as Plunkett Carter spells out: 'The thing was, if you went for a pint in Barrack Street after a match, say, a few of the Dunlop's lads were a terror for boasting about their wages – they were easy to get going about it.

'One of them might go up to the counter and throw a fifty pound note down for a pint and a drop. The barman was in on it, of course, and would be asking how much overtime he was doing and so on, and of course the reply would be, "Not at all, if I worked overtime I'd have bundles altogether." A few of them weren't shy at all.'

Red Crowley echoes Carter's point: 'A lot of lads were at the end of their careers and might have thought it was a blessing, but personally I thought it was very sad when Ford closed. I was in my thirties and I'd had my career there, as others did. The money was good, the conditions were good. Some people felt the senior management didn't try hard enough to keep it open, but those decisions hadn't been made in the Marina. We thought because Henry Ford was from Ballinascarthy that we were grand, and maybe that link helped to keep it going for so long, I don't know, but it wasn't an attitude that made any sense, really.

'There were some people who were bitter about it, but not many. A lot of people were gutted. Some went into poor health, some threw in the towel altogether. And for some of them, then, other jobs were beneath them.'

Crowley's point is well made. Former Minister Bernard Allen highlights that sometimes accommodating the expectations built up from decades in a well-paying job could be troublesome.

'The feeling was that industries like Ford and Dunlop were traditional industries – but that they weren't modern. There'd been a lack of investment in the local plants. And there was a certain lack of sympathy for those workers from some of the general public in Cork. They hadn't been shy about flaunting their wealth and the resentment probably arose from a sense of local begrudgery – that they had well-paid jobs but didn't appreciate them. Local jealousies. Generally, though, there was a sense they were too big to fail, to use a more recent phrase.'

As the men who had been made redundant began to look for alternative employment, Allen noticed an air of reality among them: 'The guys who lost their jobs turned up at the constituency clinics looking for help and guidance, but it was never vicious or anything. I'd say once the news was announced there was an acceptance: "our race is run, there's been no investment in the plant, the plant's small and there are economies of scale involved – it's inevitable."

'There was also a sense of "they've deserted us", absolutely, but the reality was the Colognes of this world were more economically viable. It would have required massive investment to bring Ford in Cork up to that standard, and the choice was either to do that or to get out. It was a no-brainer for the company. Most of the guys who were left go realised, I'd say, that they weren't going to be employed again. That it was the end of the line.'

Then there was the reputation some of the workers carried, rightly or wrongly, adds Allen.

'There was also a sense that sometimes they found it hard to get jobs because – I came across this with the gas company as well – when some of those workers took redundancy they found it hard to get work after that because they had the name of being frequent strikers. It was something similar with Ford and Dunlop, when they went for other jobs, because sometimes it was felt that they had bad habits.

'I recommended one particular guy for a job once and the personnel manager came back to me and said he wasn't sure about him because this guy had been in the gas company, and they had the name of striking frequently. So that was another barrier.

'There was no advertising jobs. You had to go hunting them out. When I got my first permanent job it was a Brother in the Mon told me there was a job in UCC, would I be interested – I went for it and got it but there was no open competition.'

At least Allen and other politicians were available. The support systems for workers made redundant are better now, but in the 1980s they were practically non-existent.

'The severance packages were generous, but I'd wonder how many of them were blown,' says Pat Casey. 'Apart from the banks, there was very little advice available. I've worked with companies which were very responsible in terms of their advice: one organisation which was taken over decided to close its Cork operation and was very assiduous about retraining, counselling, all of that. They asked me what a fair multiplier would be, in terms of weeks per year. I said eight, which was unheard of, but it was too good an opportunity to miss.

'The point was they were keen to do the right thing. They had consultants and advisers over to help out, brokers giving financial direction, all of that. And that wasn't available in the 1980s. It was a cheque and thanks.'

When those cheques ran out some of the men tried to retrain. Cónal Creedon took some AnCo courses during this period and often had former Ford and Dunlop workers in the classroom along with him.

'I can still remember some of them particularly vividly. On one of those AnCo courses it became almost a motivational exercise – "you may not get a full-time job but you could do a bit of this or that, establish a track record," all of that.

'In the first week everyone had to stand up and say who they were, what they'd done, what they were all about. And one of those men stood up – again, probably younger then than I am now – and spoke about going to school, getting a job in Ford's or Dunlop's, I can't remember which, and then he got down to the absolute minutiae. As in, "I had a locker with my name on it", and then he became emotional. He ended up saying, "I used to be someone," and the instructor asked him to sit down.'

8

Collateral Damage: Shops, Cinemas and Breweries

The uncertainty was not confined to the headline acts. The closures in the Marina might have come to national attention, but many other firms were under a cloud, and some found the 1980s a fatal decade.

For 170 years Dwyers, for instance, with its imposing frontage on Washington Street across from the courthouse, had been a mainstay in the city, a clothing and textiles firm that had employed generations of Cork people, and companies like the Lee Boot Co. further out the Western Road and, famously, the Sunbeam Wolsey factory in Blackpool.

However, world wars and revolution were not as damaging as international competition. Dwyers was in trouble by the late 1970s and in July 1981 it closed, the news making the front page of the *Examiner*, naturally enough. Also featured that day was the headline: 'Surgery To Save Shrinking Economy'.

The day before, Guinness had announced 1,000 job losses in Dublin. It was not the only brewery suffering at that time. Within twelve months a Cork institution was looking down the barrel of the gun as well.

In the mid 1970s Murphy's had 10 per cent of the national stout market and the company, full of confidence, had decided to invest in a bottling plant on the Kinsale Road. Unfortunately, various mechanical issues beset the plant from the start. It did not come on line until 1978, long after the proposed start date, and there were technical problems meeting demand almost from the beginning. Towards the end of the 1970s Murphy's approached Dutch firm Heineken, whose lager was being made in the Cork brewery, to take a direct interest in Murphy's, but Heineken declined.

The situation did not improve for the north-side brewery and a Beamish takeover looked on the cards early in the 1980s before collapsing late on in the negotiation process. Murphy's duly went into receivership in July 1982.

In the end Heineken took over the business and the brewery continued to operate, but not without significant state support. The IDA provided grant aid for equipment, for instance, and Foir Teoranta offered an interest-free loan of over £2 million for up to four years. There were further trading grants and other tax exemptions, such as an exemption on exports and a guaranteed corporation tax rate of 10 per cent per annum to the year 2000.

Beamish & Crawford, prospective rescuers of Murphy's in the early 1980s, would suffer themselves later in the decade. The south-side brewery had been in rude good health in the early 1980s when it had been linked to its neighbour across the River Lee, helped by its production of Carlsberg and Carling.

Its parent company, Carling O'Keeffe, had introduced production of Carling, which proved hugely successful for Beamish & Crawford, particularly in the Cork and Munster region; Carlsberg accounted for 12 per cent of the Irish lager market by the mid 1980s.

However, the storm clouds were visible by 1987. An Australian company, Elders IXL, bought Carling O'Keeffe and took over Beamish & Crawford. Elders owned the company that made Foster's lager and was keen on making Foster's an international brand, something that Carlsberg were understandably worried by. The Danish company was also discomfited by the prospect of its lager being made in an Elders-owned brewery in Cork.

By then, Carlsberg accounted for 40 per cent of Beamish & Crawford's output, and almost half of the 400 people in the workforce were involved in its production and distribution. Guinness, however, took over production of Carlsberg in 1988 following the Elders takeover, and Beamish & Crawford was left to produce Foster's.

The Australian lager did not take off and, as a result, the writing was on the wall for the Cork brewery. Carlsberg chief executive Michael Iuul said: 'In the end, Beamish & Crawford were the victims of big-business dealings between Canada and Australia. They got big new masters who want to Fosterise the world.'

Iuul would also point out, however, that Carlsberg Northampton produced 2 million barrels a year with 280 workers, while Beamish & Crawford produced 10 per cent of that with 400 workers: 'You can draw your own conclusions.'

In 1988 Beamish & Crawford offered early retirement to sixty workers. The rationalisation had begun.

The gloom manifested itself in another unexpected way. The city's cinemas began to vanish. In 1980 there were still six cinemas in the city. The Savoy closed in 1975 and would eventually become a shopping centre, but at the start of the 1980s the Palace, Classic, Pavilion, Lee, Capitol and Cameo cinemas were all open for business.

Various factors then came into play: the 1980s was a difficult decade generally for cinemas, given the explosion in home video use, while in Cork – for so long the preserve of RTÉ Television alone – there was suddenly more choice at home with the advent of multichannel TV. The general decline in people's spending power as a result of the downturn and job losses also had an impact, difficult though that is to measure.

In addition, the company that owned the Cork cinemas, Abbey Films, was aiming for consolidation and it made obvious sense to have one central location, modern and refurbished, rather than half a dozen different locations of varying quality. In due course, out-of-town shopping centres would be matched by cineplexes in Douglas, Ballincollig, Blackpool and Mahon, where the population was, but at a cost to the city centre. By 1990 only one cinema was open in town – the Capitol, which was then a multiscreen cinema.

Although the Everyman Palace was converted back into a theatre, for instance, the other cinema locations went through a variety of uses after closure, and the disappearance of those cinemas scarred the city even further.

If people weren't going to town to see films, this led to a general drop in footfall in the city; it meant that hundreds of people who might have been spending money there were not in town to spend that money. The downward cycle continued.

Other places barely survived. John Bruton was unsympathetic when Verolme was in trouble, but to give the Meath native his due, as Minister for Industry, Trade, Commerce and Tourism he resisted strong recommendations to the government to close the Nitrigin Éireann plant at Marino Point in Cork in 1984.

State papers showed that Bruton proposed that the NET fertiliser plant in Cork, which employed 360 people, should be allowed to continue its operations on the basis they would be reviewed in 1985. Other ministers, such as Austin Deasy, wanted NET closed on the basis of its debts – £202 million in total, including losses of £27.6 million in 1983 alone. Bruton's counter-argument was that world ammonia prices were rising, which would improve NET's prospects, and was supported by Alan Dukes, then Minister for Finance.

Bruton also sought approval in June 1984 to invest £89 million in equity in the Irish Steel plant in Haulbowline, though with the proviso that no further investment would be forthcoming, and that the government would recommend its closure if it was unable to pay its debts as they fell due. Because of the nature of the work being done at the plant, Bruton pointed out that the cost of the immediate closure of the plant would be approximately £100 million. The government was also told that that proposed £89 million investment in Irish Steel would need the approval of the European Commission, which was seeking a further examination of the company because of concerns over its viability.

The government formally approved Mr Bruton's recommend-ation to invest £89 million in Irish Steel, with £50 million of the funding made available immediately, but by December 1985 the government needed to invest another £18 million in the company.

Irish Steel had already received £6 million six months earlier, on condition that it negotiated a pay freeze with its staff until the end of 1986 and a redundancy scheme that would cut labour costs by at least 10 per cent. Just under 120 workers had availed of the redundancy package earlier that year (1985); while the pay freeze saved Irish Steel around £3 million, the redundancies provided annual savings of £1.73 million.

Bruton faced serious opposition, this time from Finance Minister Dukes, who believed the company's chances of a new investor would be improved if it was placed in liquidation rather than sold as a going concern; he added that it had already received equity of £120 million, grants of £30 million and loan guarantees of IR£35 million from the government.

'This Exchequer aid of IR£185 million has still not resulted in the company becoming viable,' Dukes said. He was also concerned that a scheme by the Minister for Energy, Dick Spring, in reducing Irish Steel's electricity costs, ran counter to EEC rules on aid to steel industries.

Bruton's argument carried the day: he pointed out that the Irish Steel workforce had accepted an austere rationalisation package, and when that was combined with a modest recovery in prices for steel, there were signs the company could become financially viable. He also pointed out it was the government's last opportunity to invest money in Irish Steel, as such aids were due to be phased out shortly by the EEC, while acknowledging that the investment of an additional £18 million could not be justified 'on strictly commercial criteria'.

There were other considerations, of course. An aide-memoire for the cabinet showed that ministers were concerned about how the possible closure of Irish Steel could impact on their chances of being re-elected to power. This document argued that the earlier the planned closure of the plant 'the further is the trauma that it causes from a general election'. The counter-argument was that if the government deferred a decision on closure, it could then argue that it had tried every possible option to save the company.

A note in July 1985 from an adviser at the Department of the Taoiseach, Patrick Honohan – now better known as the retired governor of the Central Bank – said the economic arguments on the future of Irish Steel were finely balanced.

'There is certainly no overwhelming economic argument for closure,' observed Honohan, who pointed out that it seemed likely that keeping the company open would save the Exchequer money.

Irish Steel stayed open, as did NET.

9

Patrick Street Looking like a War Zone

When Cónal Creedon left school in the late 1970s the future already looked bleak. At least it did to his teachers. Creedon makes an interesting point – the sense of doom at that point came from those who had seen the days of plenty, like the teachers, and could see how grim the times were in comparison. For him and his contemporaries, it was the only reality they knew. They got on with it.

'Looming in the background at that time was a total lack of opportunity. I remember the teachers in school saying, "there's nothing out there for you, lads! Ye'll have to take what's going." There was a sense of desperation, but the desperation was coming from the teachers rather than us.

'My generation were only snipping our apron strings and coming of age, so we had no context or points of reference of life being any other way – but I guess the teachers had seen the good days of the proverbial "job for life" when pupils joined the guards and the civil service or Ford's and Dunlop's – but those options were gone in the 1980s. At that stage I was gone to Canada.'

By the mid 1980s, when every youngster in Cork was trying to get to London or Boston and all points in between, Creedon was, in his own words, swimming against the tide.

'I was coming home. I had lived in Canada for a number of years, and at that particular moment in time, home was where my heart was, so I bought a one-way ticket. Homeward bound.'

When he did, he was surprised. The city had changed, and the shock of that change will only make sense to those who did their travelling before the age of social media.

'When you go away at a young age you bring with you a snapshot of home, but it's not like a Polaroid picture, it's like a panoramic view of your own life imprinted in your brain. This was pre-Internet, YouTube, Facebook – you couldn't just pull up a picture of Oliver Plunkett Street on your smartphone or footage of friends in a pub or a drone flying over the city. Back then you were relying solely on memory.

'And in your own mind it's easy to build home up as this magical fairyland, and sometimes that's the thing which brings you home. In my case it was different, my mother was ill, but I was glad to come home.'

Creedon can remember the walk across St Patrick's Bridge that first morning home.

'I noticed something had changed. The lamps on the bridge were broken. Along Merchant's Quay was like a mouthful of broken teeth, the iconic Gas Company building at the corner boarded up. The Pig and Whistle, The Statue Bar, Kilgrew's Toy Shop, Moriarty's Barber, Wickham's, the small hotel towards the end of the quay and the Traveller's Rest around the corner, all gone: gone and boarded up.

'Like Oisín's return from Tir Na nÓg – the Cork of my youth had changed, changed subtly yet changed dramatically. The anarchic nights down the Arc [the Arcadia Ballroom] were but a faded nostalgia of an absentee generation.'

As he left the bridge behind he set out along the main drag of St Patrick's Street.

'It was like a war zone. The flagship shops took a full broadside. Once-proud shopfronts of long-dead merchant princes were now decayed and decrepit – the Munster Arcade, the Queen's Old Castle, Egan's, Woolworth's, Burtons were abandoned, shut down and boarded up. The ESB offices were boarded up. Mangan's, a beautiful building that had that kind of curved glass at the front, curving into the doors, and outside on the footpath, Mangan's iconic clock. If you go back and look at that great old Mitchell and Kenyon footage from 1902 you can see Mangan's clock, it was such a strong brand – but panels on the glass face of the clock were broken.

'As I went on I noticed the cinemas were gone. The Capitol still had its main screen and the Mini, and I think the Lee was still going, but the Savoy had gone, the Pavilion, the Palace – the really beautiful ones were gone, amazing buildings that we really didn't appreciate until they'd gone.

'Most noticeable were the large department stores; stores from another time seemed to have undergone a mass extinction. Shops that had a huge significance for an older generation. These shops were staffed very formally – *Are You Being Served?* kind of places. I remember the old-style money tube shooting money around the shop. But those prime street-front stores were gone. Egan's, the old ecclesiastical outfitters. That was gone.

'The Victoria Hotel was kind of gone because Burgerland and Pizzaland were in there in front, and that took away some of the grandeur of the place. Woolworth's, gone.

'And they weren't just going through a change of ownership. They were gone, closed, kaput, vacant and boarded up.'

What was left behind was not in great shape.

'There were two sections of the quay that had actually fallen into the river. One was at the bottom of the Coal Quay and the other was over by where the Quay Co-op is now – but the city couldn't afford to pay to fix them. For years, literally, there were tar barrels around those gaps in the quay to warn people away. And there was no public outcry, because people knew the city was broke and there was no money to fix them. The city was falling to pieces, literally. It was happening in front of you.

'In a way it kind of reminded me of the scene in *It's A Wonderful Life*, when James Stewart comes back and the town's gone from Bedford Falls to Pottersville. It wasn't as bad as that, but it was … decayed.'

Once he settled back into Cork, Creedon noticed that prospects were so poor that people's speech patterns had literally changed as a consequence.

'I do remember when things were particularly bad at one point in the 1980s, job-wise, nothing going on at all and the old joke was that everyone was buying a train ticket to jeopardy, because it was reported in the news that there were 200 jobs in jeopardy.

'You knew instinctively, for instance, not to ask people what they were up to because if you did ask, people would just look at you blankly – the vast majority of people were up to nothing.

'At around that time I remember talking to an older man about the recession, because that's all you seemed to hear about in the news. He said to me, "this isn't a recession, a recession is something you come in and out of; this is the way it's going to be." There was that sense, that things were so bleak, that it would never change. There was an understanding that people were broke – whole families were broke – fathers, sons, mothers and daughters, all unemployed.

'There was a culture at the time of people going on AnCo courses, and I don't just mean kids fresh out of school, I mean everybody. Initially they were meant to train people into trades, but as unemployment soared and building and the trades dried up, eventually AnCo courses became less defined – and became all about keeping people off the live register rather than offering realistic employment opportunities. These courses became all about self-actualisation and confidence building because public confidence and morale were at an all-time low.'

Creedon himself did a number of the courses.

'I remember the demographics of the groups could be very interesting. There'd always be a sizeable group of people that I'd have regarded as being ancient, though they were probably younger then than I am now. Men in their forties in particular, who'd been let go from Ford's and Dunlop's. These would have been people whose lives had centered around their jobs – involved in organisations and social clubs, like the Dunlop's social club. Work outings, all of that. It became their life.

'You'd still see in the *Examiner* or the *Echo* in the death notices – whatever about someone's family or where they lived, you'd often see in brackets – late of Ford's, late of Dunlop's, because it was such a big community, and that community needs to be told that one of their own has passed away.

'That stands out for me, looking back. There was a sense of shell shock, among that older generation. It was as if the rug had been pulled out from under them. They'd realised they wouldn't be playing golf any more, or the suit was getting shiny and there was no prospect of buying a new one in the near future. They'd been getting by on the redundancy for a while but now the tap had been turned off and there was a sense of "what's going to happen now." A lot of them had dreams for their kids, hopes for their own futures, they were upwardly mobile and maybe thinking of where they'd move to later in life … and suddenly they were downwardly mobile. It had all changed, and they realised that they'd never see a "job for life" in their lifetime again. Not at their age.

'There was a sense among that age bracket of not just being redundant in terms of employment, but redundant in terms of life.'

The dynamic was different for the younger generation, however.

'It seems for my generation, the recession of the 1980s was sorta like water off a duck's back,' Creedon says. 'I'm not one to glorify the bad old days – my abiding memory of that time was walking the streets with empty pockets. It was a time when trying to turn a bob was a full-time job, and yes – it was a time of bleak bedsit land, damp and draughty flats, skip-scavenging to feed open fires, strumming guitars, AnCo courses, signing on the dole, draconian licensing laws with the associated obligatory regular police raids on semi-legal night clubs and drinking dens.

'But we did have fun back then. It's a different sorta fun when you've nothing to lose. It was a fun that sometimes straddled the black economy. A time of take what's going, and making do. We had a lot of fun with very little expectation.

'Recession and mass unemployment has a tendency to politicise and galvanise a population into collective thought and actions. Certainly for my generation, life seemed to be slightly subversive, politically we had the escalating troubles in the North – and down South we had a massively unemployed, frustrated and angry young population looking for a banner to stand under.

'There was a lot of positive action regarding the arts, gender, civil rights and various campaigns that galvanised our generation.

That sense of people doing it for themselves became a breeding ground for setting up facilities such as the Quay Co-op, the Cork Artists' Collective and Triskel Arts Centre.

'And though a decade of poverty can be a lifetime, there is something intriguing about an old town in recession – the bockety lanes and decayed grandeur, some fine old pubs and palaces that had yet to be demolished in the name of development.'

Part of the fun of the time was the music of the period, he adds – or more specifically, the Cork music of the period: 'By the time I left school in the late 1970s, Cork was rocking. The Arc was the epicentre of live music and a powerhouse of the local and national punk scene. The surge of teen spirit of that time left an indelible mark on that whole generation. Bands like Microdisney, Mean Features and Nunatax, the importance of those bands culturally only became significant to me long after the fact.

'At the time there was no great distinction between bands and audience; we all sorta knocked around together. I remember storing the odd drum kit or amp in the back hall of our house after a gig. Just like a few pool halls around the town at that time, The Arc was a place to go and meet. The music and the bands were the backdrop – if you went back another generation people would have been speaking in the same way about the young Rory Gallagher and the various beat clubs.

'My memory wasn't of people standing around discussing how brilliant or inspiring the music was; the music was the soundtrack to what was going on. But without a doubt those bands were considered very important in their own time. Not just three-chord tricksters banging out covers, it was the real thing, and we were lucky to have it – original sounds, original lyrics and their work still stands up.

'This is not me spouting out the rose-tinted nostalgia of my youth. A plethora of local bands and creatives from that time have stood the test of time and are now recognised as the touchstone of so much progressive music.

'Every generation on the cusp of adulthood needs figureheads of their own. It's a difficult age to stick your head above the parapet, and, without namechecking, there's huge credit due to those individuals.'

There was always one alternative, of course. At a time when a flight to England was a week's wages, the cheapness of the bus overcame its inconveniences.

'A lot of the people I knew who went ended up in alternative lifestyles in the arts, music, theatre. Different things. It wasn't the emigrant ship of the 1950s, the Slattery's bus to London was a tenner and you could get over and back easier. London was central and accessible. And there was a community there, word would come back and, while it mightn't have been great financially, it was a happening place.

'It was different if you went to Boston or New York. There was a different requirement from the point of view of emigration, you couldn't go to the States and just develop your artistic skills. You had to go and hit the ground running, go to work straightaway.

'But it's the same with every emigrant population. The word comes back that there's work and a bed. Pockets of friends started going together to places like London and it grew from there.'

Creedon didn't join them. After his stint in Canada he had got the travelling out of his system, and in a poetic twist, one of his AnCo courses paid off.

'I decided to stick around. Eventually I did a Start Your Own Business AnCo course; it was a new initiative set up by the government to try to get the economy going. The deal was that you would get more or less two years' dole, and within those two years you could do whatever you had to do to get up and running, but then after the two years you were on your own.

'I set up a laundrette around 1986 and gradually found myself writing short stories and radio plays. Eventually, after eleven or twelve years of clothes-washing, I decided to close the laundrette and become a full-time writer.

'And the rest – as they say – is fiction.'

In 2018, Creedon was confirmed as an adjunct professor in UCC's Department of English. The teachers were wrong: there were jobs there after all.

10

1985: Chaos

Perhaps nothing sums up the decade more than the year 1985, when the city came to international attention, but for all the wrong reasons, and seemed to tip into surreal chaos at times.

It began with the Cork 800. The 1980s saw a vogue for celebrations such as the Dublin Millennium, as cities commemorated significant if dubious milestones that had occurred centuries before. In Cork's case it was the granting of a royal charter in 1185. There were concerts and displays, commemorative fountains were built and parades held.

'It raised spirits, and that was good,' says Micheál Martin, now leader of Fianna Fáil. 'Liam Burke was Lord Mayor that time, and the fact that it brought a national focus on Cork is something that would always help, obviously. It developed a sense of community, national bodies held their meetings in Cork, all of that worked in Cork's favour.

'They were attempts to show that Cork was a different city, that it wouldn't go down.'

Still, the beginning was not auspicious. An air show was planned at Cork Airport to kickstart the celebrations, and thousands turned up to be entertained by the derring-do of the pilots who had flown in from overseas.

Unfortunately, the fog was too thick for the planes to be seen, so the show was cancelled. Despite this, thousands of people still came to the airport and flooded into the terminal and the viewing areas, though there was nothing to see.

Which in itself is a commentary on the time.

A shadow hung over other transport options as well. B & I had pulled out of the Cork–Wales ferry route in 1983, and there was wrangling at the cabinet table over whether to offer another company financial support to run a summer service in 1985.

Swansea Cork Car Ferries had been set up in June 1984 but it needed state funding if it were to provide a summer service in 1985. State papers released thirty years later show that Communications Minister Jim Mitchell opposed a subsidy but also acknowledged the economic challenges Cork was facing. With the Cork 800 celebrations also starting, he was prepared to okay a once-off subsidy of £500,000 to help get the service off the ground.

Finance Minister Alan Dukes opposed the subsidy, estimating that the losses of running a service between Cork and Swansea could be as high as £1 million – which the state would be under pressure to cover. Minister for Tourism John Bruton also opposed the subsidy, saying he was more concerned about funding for improvements at other ports like Rosslare and Dún Laoghaire.

Nevertheless, Mitchell won the day: the new service was offered a subsidy of up to 40 per cent of any losses up to maximum of £500,000.

Come the summer there were local elections for the first time in seven years. On 21 June 1985, Bernie Murphy won a seat on the city council, and two days later Air India Flight 132 went down off the Cork coast. The following month saw thousands travel to a grotto near Ballinspittle to see a statue of the Blessed Mary move. The three events all drew international attention, little of it particularly flattering.

Bernie Murphy, who carried a sandwich board around town and was regarded as a harmless character, saw his campaign for a corporation seat treated with initial scepticism by the bookies. The betting on Murphy had opened at 50/1, but within days the odds had shortened radically and by election day, 21 June, he was being quoted at 9/4; Liam Cashman would later tell the *Examiner* that the biggest single bet made was £100 at 33/1 odds and added that some bets had come in from the legal profession. In the end he won 1,242 votes and was elected on the eleventh count.

Murphy was fifty when elected and, according to his own campaign literature, had been on the streets since the age of fifteen. He was functionally illiterate.

'I hated every minute of it,' says Pat Casey, then a reporter for the *Examiner*. 'I didn't cover a lot of it but I was involved to some extent working on it. I thought it was an ugly exploitation of somebody by people who had made very little contribution to the city, by and large.

'I have no respect for those puppeteers who were involved. They took someone who was vulnerable, really, and pushed him out in front for their own amusement. They could weave all sorts of excuses in terms of a protest vote, but those who dealt with Bernie in City Hall knew exactly what the cost was, eventually, to him.

'It was a very ugly episode and reflects very badly on those people, as far as I'm concerned. A senior City Hall official told me that Bernie couldn't read the notice on the door to tell him where his committee meetings were.

'There was a meeting outside the Victoria Hotel at one point during the campaign, music, speeches, and Bernie came on stage and delivered a few sentences he'd been given, and … no. It was terrible. I felt it was a sad period. In fairness to the *Echo* and the *Examiner*, it was an election and had to be covered, but the newspaper didn't give it the oxygen they were looking for.'

Kathleen Lynch echoes Casey's point: 'There have always been antiheroes, and we see that more now than ever. He was probably the first of those. The modern antihero is usually articulate. Bernie wasn't. He was exploited, he was front-page news, and he wasn't ridiculed in council, but he was definitely treated with disdain. I felt "this man was elected the same as everybody else, it might not have been his choice but nobody has a right to treat him badly".

'And he was treated appallingly on occasion. He wasn't capable of defending himself. At times I think he might not have realised what was happening, and I have to say I felt the cheek of some people – councillors – to treat anybody like that. It was a sorry episode but Bernie himself always acted with dignity and never disrespected anyone, which is something you couldn't always say of his supposed betters. That wasn't the case with every councillor, but there were times you'd be thinking, "don't do this".

'He was a pawn. The people behind him were bright, intelligent people but it wasn't even a case of getting someone to articulate a point of view. It was a group deciding that it was beneath them to try to get elected; getting elected to this *Ballymagash*-style local council was beneath them, but it was okay for Bernie. They were going to show people up in the same way. That's abuse.'

At first glance, given the hammer blows to the city over the previous twelve months, some form of protest vote seems entirely explicable. Dissatisfaction with the status quo, the traditional political parties, would hardly have been a shock. Yet Murphy's election was regarded by many observers as a far more cynical exercise, as noted above. Why?

It was suggested at the time that the legal profession was behind Murphy's election. Bernard Allen, then a TD, has no doubt about it.

'A clever prank, but at the same time, there was another side to it. There was a disenchantment with authority, the City Council and its outgoing members were seen as part of the establishment, and the disenchantment manifested itself in a protest vote.

'Of course, the people behind Bernie Murphy put him up in my ward, North Central – they recognised the disenchantment that was there and they used Bernie to get that. I remember having a confrontation in the Imperial Hotel one evening around that time with someone who was involved in Bernie's camp.

'Some years afterwards he apologised, and said he was sucked into it, but it happened, the result came out, and I moved on, and forgot about it. What I did learn was that the legal profession has deep-rooted influence on the political system, and that was an example where they felt they could have a cheap go at me.'

At that period Allen was at loggerheads with the legal profession, its lack of accountability in particular ('which still exists'), and the fact that the government was very reluctant to do anything about it.

'As an example, take one of the Solicitors (Amendment) Acts during that decade – what came out at the end was totally different to what was set out in the Second Stage debate: the Law Society got enough pressure on to dilute, in particular, the question of lay participation in the disciplinary system – something they still oppose, by the way – and it remained self-regulating.

'And any area that's self-regulated is open to abuse. That day should be gone, and you'd imagine now it would be gone, but in the 1980s and 1990s the legal profession ruled the roost, really.'

Allen's counter-argument is that if the energy put into Bernie Murphy's election had been put into the civic life of the city, more would have been achieved.

'Those people wouldn't have wasted their time – as they saw it – getting involved in local politics, in creating change. Their expenses would have been too small. As it was, they were happy to be hurlers on the ditch, criticising what was being done without contributing – in fact, they were functioning as roadblocks rather than bringing about reform.

'The purpose of running Bernie was to get at me and to teach me a lesson. The success of the exercise came down to their cleverness and also to that disenchantment – which they could exploit and did.'

Murphy's election was seized upon overseas. The *Los Angeles Times* ran a feature on him which included a visit to his lodgings, where he was frying sausages, while a San Francisco newspaper columnist brought him to that city for a visit which provided plenty of copy as well: one of his speeches ran to thirty seconds.

Murphy later ran for the Dáil twice but did not get in. In time he returned to his old life, strolling Oliver Plunkett Street and the walkways of the English Market, tapping old acquaintances for a couple of bob.

The news that a Boeing 747 had gone down in Irish airspace broke early on 23 June. The Air India flight was en route from Montreal to London when it disappeared from radar screens at 7.15 a.m.

Within two hours, a passing ship had found wreckage and bodies in the ocean 120 miles off the Cork coast: the 307 passengers and 22 crew had died when a bomb went off on board.

The Navy, Air Corps, local emergency services and Cork Regional Hospital (now Cork University Hospital) were stretched to the limit: the LE *Aisling* was trying to retrieve bodies from the deep ocean and there was not enough room in the hospital for those bodies. In time, Sikh separatists would be blamed for the bomb but the immediate aftermath was chaotic, with helicopters flying in the bodies to the hospital in Wilton, where the temporary morgue was under armed guard.

Michael Farber was a journalist with the *Montreal Gazette* at the time, and his editor immediately despatched him to Cork.

'I took the same flight route as the Air India flight the night after it crashed, into Heathrow, and then I and another journalist went on to Cork – right to the press centre, where we worked and worked. Suddenly it's midnight in Cork, and I've filed my story, and I realise I don't have a place to stay. You're on the go for thirty hours and you forget about accommodation, that stuff.'

One of the telephone operators who was working at the airport tried to get Farber a place to stay, but everywhere was booked. Eventually the operator said she had friends with a spare bedroom. She called them.

'They agreed to put me up for ten pounds a night, I think,' says Farber. 'The man of the house had been a sailor, and was an affable guy, but his wife's accent was so heavy I couldn't understand it, but they were great. They took me in and put me up for practically nothing. Six days later I had to leave, so I told them I'd be off. I was flying out of Shannon to Boston on the way home, I'd be renting a car and so on.

'No, no, the man of the house wouldn't hear of that. He said to give him what I was going to give the car hire firm and he'd drive me, that way I wouldn't have to worry about driving on the left and so on. That was okay but we stopped in every pub between Cork and Shannon. I'd never had Murphy's before, and I'd describe Murphy's as what Guinness would taste like if Guinness was actually good. It's not even close. We got to Shannon, he pushed me out of the car and gave me a six pack of Murphy's. Which I took on the plane, weaving slightly.'

On a more serious note, Farber was impressed by his time in Ireland: 'My impression of Cork was not negative at all. It was incredibly positive. A press centre was set up in the airport and they were most accommodating. It was great work in trying circumstances and two things impressed me in particular. One was the dignity with which the people who came to Cork were treated – the families of those who died, Canadian and Indian. The warmth with which they were received, and the compassion – that stuck with me. It started with how the victims' families comported themselves – with great dignity. Then it was how they were greeted in Ireland, with huge respect and dignity. It was my first real experience of Ireland and it was overwhelmingly positive, given the terrible circumstances. Maybe it was because of those circumstances, the worst you could imagine, that people rose to the occasion and it brought out the best in everyone – the Indians comporting themselves with that incredible dignity, and being met in Ireland with huge kindness and generosity and compassion.

'Obviously it was a horrendous tragedy, all those lives lost, but what I took from it was the great respect of the local people. Cork was an innocent bystander in this and I thought its response to something that was beyond its control was magnificent. Cork, to me, got an A plus on that occasion.'

Farber was not alone. The Canadian Prime Minister, Brian Mulroney, wrote to the Lord Mayor of Cork just five weeks later:

It is with deep admiration that I write to express gratitude to the residents of Cork for the assistance offered to the families and friends of the Air India Flight victims.

The generosity of time that they have given so freely and their humanitarian spirit have been a true source of comfort to all those who suffered the sudden loss of loved ones. I know that all Canadians share the sense of the overwhelming human tragedy of the victims of Flight 182, but they have also been touched by the way the residents of Cork have opened up their hearts to absorb the grief of this painful human experience.

It was July when reports started to filter out of Ballinspittle, near Kinsale, of a statue moving in a grotto on the road out of the village.

As a marker of the desperation and chaos of the times some form of religious hysteria was hardly surprising, and though statues would soon be described as moving all over Ireland, Ballinspittle would become synonymous with the phenomenon.

Crowds of up to 10,000 people began to descend on the village from across the country, giving the locals plenty of headaches when it came to accommodation and traffic control. Pat Casey remembers pointing the car that direction one evening: 'It was light relief in one way but it was serious to the people going down and praying at the grotto. We went down one night after *Nighttown*, around two in the morning, to do some investigative journalism.

'It was a misty night, and there were hundreds there despite the time. All praying. There was a small hill opposite the grotto so I went over there to look properly at the statue. To be honest, I thought it was going to fall off the plinth, it was moving so much. I said "what the … this can't be happening". It wasn't moving. It was rocking on the plinth from where I was standing. I'd been laughing as we drove down, but then …

'When I lined up the statue with a tree or a telegraph pole, there wasn't a move. I was happy then it was an optical illusion, that somebody wasn't trying to get a message to me, but whatever the combination of mist and angle and light, it certainly looked like it was moving. That gave me a fright, but I was relaxed enough when we left that it wasn't as active as I first thought. If you were of that mind and you saw it, you'd embrace it.'

Kathleen Lynch's view is similar: 'It was a time of chaos and poverty – we see it now in the Eastern Bloc – and in that kind of time people turn to something they see as magical. I think you needed to begin with a certain element of desperation or belief, or both.

'I went down and looked and sorry, no. All I could think of was that for someone who genuinely believed there was something out there, they'd want to be annoyed if this was how they were regarded or represented. It was a time of crisis. People were desperate for some semblance of hope, and I think that's what Ballinspittle was.'

There wasn't even succour on the playing fields: heavily favoured to overcome Galway and advance to a fourth All-Ireland hurling final in four years, Cork lost out to the westerners on a dank, rainy day in Croke Park. Another blow.

Pat Fitzgerald came out of UCC in the middle of the decade. His experience was typical: get out, and get out fast.

'I probably never understood the despair in the city during the early 1980s because I went to UCC in 1981 to do a B. Comm and was going to the States in the summers, making enough to come back and enjoy college. I don't remember that despair because when we came out of college, every single one of us was leaving Ireland – never mind the city, the country – apart from those who wanted to study accountancy or who were going to KPMG and Deloitte, the big accountancy firms. The rest of us went to London, basically, so I never had that sense of "there are no jobs here" because a huge number of us never even tried to get a job in Cork.'

It was not all bad news, though. A new shopping centre opened in the city towards the end of 1985 in the Paul Street area, which had been near derelict for years.

On the same day, Bishop Lucey Park was opened on the Grand Parade, although the name ruffled feathers in the Protestant community, which had donated part of the grounds used. There was a good take-up of the shopping units in Paul Street, reported local auctioneers, but the city was lacking one vital ingredient as December approached: a long-running ESB strike, which had led to violence on the picket lines near Douglas in October, meant there were no Christmas lights in the city that year.

11

Beyond the Pale: a Second City

Any example will do. At the height of the Ballinspittle moving statues, in the summer of 1985, then-government press secretary Peter Prendergast was asked about the phenomenon, and he was quoted as saying 'three-quarters of the country is laughing heartily' at the reports.

Prendergast did not detail where the devout quarter of the country was – presumably the Munster region – but his aside was taken by some in Cork to reflect a Dublin-based ignorance, or indifference, to what was going on in the southern capital.

This was partly a tribal reaction, one which superseded common sense or, for that matter, the available evidence. Gerald Goldberg, one of the art collectors mentioned by Theo Dorgan, was also a local politician of note throughout the 1980s, and the most visible representative of Cork's then-dwindling Jewish community.

At one point in an interview Goldberg was asked – rather delicately – if he had ever faced prejudice.

'Oh yes. Yes, indeed,' said Goldberg, adding, 'In Dublin, they always have the knife out for the Cork man.'

More seriously, the dislocation was a reality in the 1980s, and in specific cases the lack of interest from the capital was a real concern. Niall Hartnett can recall union anger in Dunlop when the ITGWU head office, based in Dublin, did not engage more fully with the talks as the factory closed.

'The factory was managed locally. The Cork–Dublin beef would have been on the union side. The head of the ITGWU, John Carroll, made no effort to come to Cork at that time, and that didn't help. I know my father would have felt they could have done more, and the feeling in Cork – about everything – that if this was happening in Dublin they'd do something, that was certainly true in this case. But there was a feeling, certainly, that they didn't care in Dublin.'

Toddy O'Sullivan was a TD throughout the 1980s: he met the same lack of curiosity in the capital when the squeeze came on in Cork.

'Lots of people in Dublin didn't realise the importance of those industries in particular, Ford, Dunlop, Verolme, which is not to forget the other smaller companies – catering, building, all of those – because they closed as well. But there was a sense that it was far away. The Dunlop workers had a sit-in in the Dublin offices – I had friends there – but it was frustrating because the decisions had been made overseas. Local management had no control over that.'

Another TD broke that down further. In Bernard Allen's view there were two sides to the attitude in the capital: a disregard for what was happening three hours' drive away, and a focus on events which took place between the canals.

'In Dublin, in the Dáil, we were regarded as whingers looking for a handout. I remember talking to a senior minister about Verolme needing assistance, and all he could say was the work practices were poor there and what did we expect, state aid for the shipbuilding industry? There was very little sympathy.

'What I noticed when I went to Dublin was the networking. There was none of that for Cork businesses – or businesses in other areas – but you'd be at a launch or an event and the civil servants, politicians, business people, journalists, all of them would be networking away.'

When there were moves to churn out more dentists in Dublin, Allen saw the mechanism at work up close: 'It was there with the controversy over the dental school in Cork. A super dental school was to be built in Dublin, but a manpower survey done at the time showed that made no sense, that the demand wasn't there for dentists and ancillary services. The fallout would have been the closure of the Cork dental hospital, but as it went on you could see how that particular issue revealed how business was done.

'People from Trinity and UCD would be meeting Ministers and senior civil servants day in day out, and the deal would be done informally: it'd be presented as a fait accompli in terms of legislation or policy, but the details would have been worked out over a pint in Doheny and Nesbitt's or coffee in Buswell's Hotel.

'If you were a TD from outside the Pale then you were a Tuesday to Thursday politician really, and the real work was being done in Dublin over the weekend, networking at functions, dinner parties, all of that. If it were the two of us, say, we'd meet up informally and agree the points, I'd send you a memo on that or whatever, and it rolled on from there.

'So you were at a major disadvantage in that sense. Those kinds of things had TDs and ministers promoting and advocating for them, and even if they were from outside Dublin, by definition they were spending a lot of time in Dublin where they had their ears bent by local experts. That happened over and over. It bit even deeper because there was no redistribution mechanism and commercial rates were low, particularly in Cork, when it came to funding local authorities.'

Micheál Martin agrees with Allen on the remoteness of the capital.

'That's a long-running thesis, and there was a Dublin-centric view of life. There's a factor of greater networking going on in Dublin which is consistent and constant, and which excludes the regions – among civil servants and politicians. And that is an issue. Everyone now agrees we should have alternatives to Dublin but everyone there is reinforcing each others' prejudices.'

Sometimes politicians ventured outside the Pale and were brought up against the truth. When poet Theo Dorgan got married in the 1980s he did not let his opportunity pass.

'I borrowed the Starry Plough from Connolly Hall – with their permission – to fly from Blackrock Castle for the reception. I wanted to see it fly over one castle once.

'Anyway, John Bruton was at the wedding. He was the friend of a friend and at the time he was a minister – I remember the Special Branch man driving him into the forecourt. At one point in the evening he was up on the battlements looking down the river and said, "I never knew Cork was so industrialised," and my brother Chris was going past and overheard him.

'"Oh yeah," said Chris, "There's Ford's, Dunlop's, Verolme … wait, no there isn't, Minister."

'And what struck me was that here was a government minister and what had happened hadn't gotten through to him. It had gotten through to Gurranabraher and Churchfield, and Turner's Cross and Ballyphehane, and Blackpool, but not to Dublin.

'I think that was the moment I realised 'there are no guardian angels any more; there are no miracle solutions." Now Apple came a a kind of a miracle solution, but that came at a time when people had come to mistrust saviours – in fact, they weren't regarded as saviours. People's view was "what are the terms, how long are you here for?"

'The truth, that there were no more jobs for life, was delivered to Cork by two big multinational companies. It was delivered brutally, but the lesson was learned quickly. People also learned that your job could be taken, and your money could be taken, but it didn't mean that your dignity could be taken. You could rely on your imagination, and you could do valuable work, and not just for pay. At one stage myself and Mick Hannigan were paying ourselves less from the Film Festival than we would have gotten from the dole, but what did we want? We wanted to keep the festival going and we were getting satisfaction out of life.

'That was the idea, that what matters is that your life must matter. That you're not living to work, but working to live. That idea was slow spreading in the culture, but it always comes in concrete form, and the concrete form in Cork was that anything could go if Ford and Dunlop could go. As a result, you had to ask yourself, what do I really want? It was a tough lesson.'

The brutality of the lesson also reinforced Dorgan's point about self-reliance and became incorporated, in some ways, into the world view in Cork.

The notion that nothing was truly stable and permanent was only part of it; the message that the city was on its own was equally strong, and one which tended, eventually, to be associated with one individual in Dublin more than others.

12

Haughey and Cork

Years later Cork took its revenge. In 1999, when Jack Lynch died, a state funeral was held in Cork for the former Taoiseach. The Mass itself was celebrated at the North Cathedral, a hundred yards from Lynch's childhood home near Shandon.

As dignitaries arrived at the church gates they were accompanied by civil servants as they walked the thirty yards or so across the car park to the church steps, watched by a large crowd of locals, who had assembled at the gates and along the Shandon Street side fence.

When former Taoiseach Charles Haughey arrived there was a chilly silence from the crowd as he made his way into the church – where, to some hilarity, he was seated alongside one of his old sparring partners, Dessie O'Malley.

But when his state car joined the cortège after the Mass there was no mistaking the crowd's reaction: scattered jeering was audible from locals along the route through the city to the cemetery.

Even allowing for Lynch's iconic status in Cork, it was a striking show of distaste. But then again, many Cork people could still remember the 1980s, which were then recent enough history. Haughey had been Taoiseach on three different occasions (1981, 1982 and from 1987 to the end of the decade) and many of those in the crowd no doubt remembered in particular the feeling that Haughey had turned his back on the city when it needed help.

Were they correct?

Lynch had fired Haughey from the cabinet in 1970, of course, as a result of the Arms Crisis, and Haughey had spent years in the political wilderness as a result. When he finally took over from Lynch as Fianna Fáil leader in 1979 it was a surprise, as many observers had expected George Colley, Lynch's heir apparent, to take that role.

To say Lynch and Haughey did not enjoy a warm relationship would be a considerable understatement. While Haughey was party leader there was a certain amount of airbrushing of Lynch from the party history, for instance, and it certainly made sense to Cork people to infer an accompanying antipathy on Haughey's part as a result towards Lynch's home place.

Those living outside the capital often feel that no matter what the arena – politics, industry, sport – Dublin exerts a magnetic pull in terms of resources and exposure; that feeling can become stronger the further one gets from the Liffey, and in a time of crisis it is easy to understand the grip that feeling exerts.

Haughey was not the only leader seen by Cork people in the 1980s as being detached from reality – or more specifically, detached from Cork reality, perhaps.

In the flurry of general elections during the early 1980s, a story circulated widely that Fine Gael leader Garret FitzGerald had been deeply moved by the fellow feeling expressed on Leeside with the Polish trade union Solidarity – then battling the communist regime in that country – remarking on the number of Polish flags on show in support of the union members.

The red-and-white flags were, in fact, being flown ahead of an All-Ireland hurling final featuring Cork, though the cursory reference in FitzGerald's autobiography to Cork's travails at that time tend to suggest that southern issues were not a high priority for him.

However, some of Haughey's strokes were, if not blatantly anti-Cork, blithely unsympathetic: when the Talbot car factory in Dublin was closed during the early 1980s, the workers were promised by Haughey that their wages would be paid by the state. The contrast with Ford, Dunlop and Verolme could hardly have been more stark.

Haughey's antipathy towards Cork also had an immediate and obvious basis which had very little to do with Jack Lynch. Whatever his feelings about his former boss were, Haughey certainly did not like coming to Cork because he disliked dealing with the local media, who invariably gave him a hard time when he visited the city.

The reason was simple. The physical distance between Dublin and Cork also preserved the separation of journalist and politician. Lobby journalists and political correspondents in Leinster House were seeing Haughey and other politicians almost every day: in the Dáil bar, in the cafe, along the corridors. Attacking a taoiseach or minister personally in a morning newspaper or on a radio show might lead to an awkward enough encounter over coffee and scones in the restaurant that afternoon.

Haughey supporters might claim – and did claim at the time
– that media outlets didn't hold back in their criticism of him,
though the obvious retort to that argument is that it took many
years for the sources of funding which propped up his lifestyle to
be identified. That was an area worthy of investigation which was
not subjected to much journalistic scrutiny for decades.

On the other hand, when Haughey came to Cork on official
business, the politician–journalist relationship was quite different.
He was usually tackled by the same journalists – Donal Musgrave
and Val Dorgan from the *Cork Examiner* and Dick Hogan of *The
Irish Times* among them – and because they were based in Cork,
not Leinster House, they didn't hold back with their questioning,
which tended to be a good deal more forthright than Haughey
was accustomed to.

Gerry Wrixon, former President of UCC, has a vivid
memory of Haughey being asked directly on one of his trips to
Cork about his sources of revenue, for instance. The man who
asked that question, Donal Musgrave, was an experienced, well-
established journalist in the 1980s and he makes no bones about
Haughey – and the background to his own relationship with the
politician.

'We wanted stories, and he got a roasting every time he came
to Cork,' says Musgrave. 'And I had a personal history with
Haughey, too. When I was a young reporter with the *Irish Press*
in the 1960s there was a foot-and-mouth outbreak in Britain,
and the government of the time issued a plea to emigrants not to
come home that Christmas, as that was the prime time for the
disease to spread.

'I got a tip-off from the Irish Embassy in London that friends
of Neil Blaney [then a high-profile Donegal TD] were going
home from England to Dublin by boat and would criss-cross the
country on the way back to Donegal – and that Haughey was

behind it. I wrote the story for the *Irish Press*, the *Evening Press* and the *Sunday Press*, but nothing appeared. Soon after that I was at a do in the Irish Embassy in London, and Haughey was there.

'When I was introduced to him he said, "Ah, Mr Musgrave, I understand you've been taking an undue interest in my affairs – don't forget the paper you're working for."'

It was not meant as banter and Musgrave did not take it as such. It stuck in his memory for what it was.

'A direct threat, and I never forgot that, so I had an axe to grind which the other lads didn't. He hated coming to Cork and resented the questions, which were perfectly reasonable questions on policy. His officials would try to interrupt and we'd brush them aside, all of that.'

Other circumstances did not commend Cork to Haughey as a happy hunting ground. Musgrave can also recall a particular Haughey visit which didn't end well for the politician.

'John O'Connell, who owns Murray's Tackle Shop in Patrick Street, was the receiver for Sunbeam, the textile company, when it closed down, and Haughey paid a visit to the factory, which could have been during an election campaign.

'While in Sunbeam, Haughey took a particular interest in one painting in the boardroom, and while John O'Connell could see he coveted it for his collection, he also decided that whatever he got out of the visit, it wouldn't be that painting.

'John gave him a parcel to mark his visit, but the parcel contained socks, not the painting. It didn't go down at all well, either. And I think it was the Jack Lynch factor as well – the "uncrowned king" aspect of Lynch's reputation, which would have been tangible in Cork. Haughey had his own apparatchiks who'd have been on the anti-Lynch side, and Lynch was a strong factor, certainly.'

Gerry Wrixon concurs with Musgrave, though not perhaps on the exact cause of that antipathy. The academic had a different relationship with Haughey, one that was founded on a very different basis from that of the local media, but he agrees the politician's dislike for Cork wasn't an urban myth.

'He did have a lack of interest in Cork, whether that was down to Jack Lynch or whatever else, I don't know. He didn't talk to me about that, but I had that impression. For instance, there was a fuss around that time about a proposed river crossing for the Lee – would it be under the river or over it, that kind of thing. People couldn't agree. And that annoyed him, I remember, that people couldn't come to an agreement on that. He liked people who could make up their minds and make decisions.'

Wrixon, with a PhD in electrical engineering, had first come across Haughey in the 1970s when he had slipped out of his particular area of expertise and into what was a truly alternative field at the time. The politician had taken notice.

'I was always interested in solar energy,' says Wrixon. 'And in UCC the electrical engineering department had gotten a couple of grants from the EU to look at new types of solar cells. I gave a talk at some point in Dublin on solar energy, and not long after, I got a call from Charlie Haughey, who was a minister at the time. He hadn't been at the talk but must have read the programme, or an account of the proceedings, and he asked me to come and see him the next time I was in Dublin.'

The two men met up and hit it off. Haughey was talking about his island off the coast of Kerry, Inishvickillane, and in particular the energy sources on the island.

It was an area where Wrixon could help out: 'He was saying he was interested in getting sources of renewable energy out there, would I be interested in doing something in that line and so on. I went down there to have a look and eventually he decided to get some solar energy to power various things in the house – he worked with other people on wind energy, which was subsequent to my work there.

'This took a couple of years to sort out, so I developed a rapport with him over that time. Personally, I thought him a very smart, incisive person.'

Wrixon would also have a front-row seat when it came to Haughey's duels with the fourth estate on Leeside.

'When we had an opening or some kind of ceremony at one stage in UCC I invited Haughey down, and I specifically remember Donal Musgrave and a number of other reporters came to meet him, and their first question was "perhaps you could tell us about your wealth, Mr Haughey?"

'I can't remember his answer, but it was obvious he was used to questions like that. I didn't know anything about that side of things.'

Wrixon was impressed with Haughey's decisiveness: 'He was interested in the future and was a good ideas person. Quite often you have the feeling a politician is just in a state of stasis, particularly if he or she can't find consensus: to me he was more of a leader. He seemed to have good ideas about various things. From that point of view I got a good impression of him – I didn't know about all the other stuff that came out later. When it came to the solar power on the island, he paid for everything himself, certainly.'

Throughout the 1980s there was a belief in Cork that a serious, dominating politician such as Jack Lynch would have been a huge asset to the city, but in retirement the former Taoiseach kept a very low profile, and Fitzgerald and Haughey were the big beasts of the time.

Despite the distance and apparent dislike, however, Haughey would facilitate one crucial development on Leeside in the face of strong lobbying from Dublin and Limerick, a development in which Wrixon's relationship with the politician would prove hugely beneficial. For all the distrust many people on Leeside felt for him, Haughey's decisiveness – gently, or not so gently pushed, by Gerry Wrixon – would in time enhance Cork considerably as an industrial location and education hub.

13

'Ardnósach': UCC in the Eighties

Nowadays if you come to Cork by some of its main approach roads you will see a chocolate-brown signpost with an impressionistic squiggle and an insistent caption: 'Cork, a university city since 1845.'

Before the regional technical colleges became institutes of technology, and ahead of the promotion of the national institutes of higher education in Limerick and Galway, this was a boast well worth making. Within the Republic, only Trinity College, University College Dublin and University College Galway were in competition with UCC as universities.

The college on the Western Road was a significant presence in the city as a result. It was a major employer, for instance, and an access point for expertise across a wide range of fields likely to help a city in distress on any number of fronts – economics and technology being obvious examples.

For depressed areas of the city – and there was no shortage of those – it could offer young people a pathway upwards through education while, from the outside, its presence marked Cork apart within the country. The city's reputation was boosted by its presence; UCC underlined Cork's bona fides as the country's second city.

And yet. Town and gown separation was a very real phenomenon. Take the experience of one bright youngster.

'It was a decade of contrasts for me,' says Micheál Martin. 'I did my Leaving Certificate in 1978 and went to UCC that year, the first in my family to go to college. My father was a bus driver, we didn't get grants, but we managed it. The background was getting greyer, getting into the 1980s – you'd had the oil crisis of the late 1970s, and the 1980s weren't an improvement, but I was going to college and all the excitement associated with that. Outside that – my older brother Sean couldn't get a job when he got out of school, jobs were so, so scarce.

'There was no such thing as an internship or a placement, getting in somewhere for six months with a view to being taken on. Part-time jobs in bars and so on, that was about it. We were lucky in that we got jobs in a bakery – we had cousins in bakeries and myself and Sean and Paudie, my other brothers, got jobs in Mother's Pride and then in Fitzgerald's out on the Tramore Road. And that financed us in terms of pocket money in college and so on, but full-time jobs were scarce.'

By his own admission, Martin took a while to get to grips with college life – in and out of the lecture theatre.

'I found UCC hard enough in terms of integrating early on. I was eighteen, nineteen, living at home – and involved in committees with Nemo Rangers even then. I'd leave college every day and head home, and wasn't really integrating. Most of the time I was doing what most lads did – sadly enough, we'd go to the ceilis a lot of the time in Áras na Dige, the Irish-language place on the Mardyke, because it was run by Seamus Lankford who taught us in Críost Rí.

'Sometimes we'd head to Chandra's nightclub, wander to a chipper in Douglas Street and haul yourself out of bed for a junior football match with Nemo the next morning. Work it all out of the system, but the point is, life went on.'

In common with many students – particularly those living at home – Martin did not settle down in UCC until he had a year completed.

'In second year I opened up a bit and got involved more. I think it happens a lot with students, that it takes them that year or so to get their bearings, maybe, and I discovered the Philosoph, which became the social outlet. You'd go to that for the debates on a Saturday night, pints after that in the College Bar and a house party somewhere. Simple enough pleasures.'

While in UCC, Martin became more politically involved: it was an eventful time, after all.

'I got elected to the City Council in 1985, but the political backdrop going back a couple of years before that, really, was the hunger strikes in 1981.

'My first ever public speech was in the old "Rest" canteen in UCC, packed with students from Fianna Fáil, Fine Gael, Sinn Féin, guys who wanted to do this, that or the other – I can't even remember what the substance of the motion was that was being discussed, but I was up on a table myself getting excited and making a speech on the issue.

'We had a strong Cumann in UCC at the time, and I ran for President of the Students' Union in 1982; one thing I remember is Joe Duffy, then President of the Union of Students of Ireland, coming down to persuade the UCC Students' Union to remain in the USI, and I joined him – against my own executive, who wanted to leave the USI. We failed spectacularly to keep the union in the USI, though I got to know Joe as a result, but the hunger strikes were the big political events of my time in college.'

Beyond those national issues there were local concerns. Martin became editor of two college magazines and ended up interviewing P. J. Mara and Vincent Browne, among others, while he held those positions. On the front of one of the issues of those magazines was a photograph of local politicians Paud Black and John Blair.

'Paud Black was Lord Mayor at the time – 1981 – and he was pelted with flour on Patrick Street in a student protest about fees. Being the editor the following year I remember urging students to be responsible and not to pelt the lord mayor, but you were divorced from the city, you were in your own bubble above in the college.

'But that has always been part of it. In modern planning, the city's getting better at integrating UCC, and it's a hobby horse of mine. It's an education city and should be marketed as such, and strongly, but there was also a touch of the *ardnósach* about the college – "we are the gown", that kind of thing.

'In fairness, the NMRC represented a renaissance in the city and Haughey got that early on.'

The National Microelectronics Research Centre was at the embryonic stage and though it was a harbinger of a more integretated college, the attitude Martin identifies as 'we are the gown', is a sore point with another politician. Bernard Allen represented the north side of the city for thirty years in the Dáil. He acknowledges what the NMRC did for the city reputationally but with a caveat.

'I'm not being negative but I think in deprived areas of Cork it had no influence whatsoever. But in developing Cork as an attractive base for new investment it helped, reputationally it helped.

'CIT has done a massive amount, but my only disappointment with it and UCC is that neither delivered on their promises to put campuses, or a campus, on the north side of the city. A campus on its own wouldn't have resolved that many things, because it was access to third level that needed to be addressed rather than a physical presence, but it would have expressed a vote of confidence in the north side of the city.'

The need for a vote of confidence is best expressed by the attitude of one academic: 'A few years ago I discussed the need for a campus on the north side with a senior academic,' says Allen. 'He said, "why would we want to be going up there? It wouldn't be good for the image of the institution." That still exists. For some of them the River Lee is like the Rio Grande.

'My biggest disappointment is Our Lady's Hospital and how that wasn't developed. It's not just the big, long building in front, but the entire grounds stretching all the way back up the hill to Knocknaheeny – I don't know how many acres are involved in total. There was an agreement that UCC would take that over, and in 1994 UCC were offered everything on the site along with £40 million, a lot of money at the time. That was the amount, a consultant's report stated, needed to get the place up to scratch, and that was offered; there was a proposal to move the medical school up there but Michael Mortell, then the President, was against it and swayed the governing body against it, and the place has been a scar on the north side ever since.

'It has cost hundreds of thousands in security, when the department of medicine moving up there would have lifted the entire north-west of the city. The dean of medicine at the time was a progressive guy – his vision wasn't just to have a medical school, but to have departments of radiography, chiropody, biomedical, incubation units for biotechnology, all of those there.'

Allen contrasts the modern sprawl of UCC with what could have been achieved just across the river: 'The college was so shortsighted and, in my view, had no social conscience. Ever since it has developed willy-nilly along the Western Road and College Road, wiping out residential areas – going out to Curraheen and building there, the Maltings, developing all over the place.

'The UCC students' union even protested against the prospect of going to the north side, by the way. I said at the time that departments in Our Lady's Hospital would only be five minutes from the main UCC campus – I was gilding the lily a little, it was five minutes from the Mardyke, but that's part of the UCC campus. There were European elections at the time and I was thinking of running, and someone said that if I could get from UCC to Our Lady's Hospital in five minutes I should be running for the Olympics and not Europe.'

Our Lady's Hospital is still there, stark along the horizon. Still undeveloped.

'It reminds me every day of what could be there,' says Allen. 'Think of the spin-off industries, the employment opportunities for local people … the money was on offer and they didn't avail of the opportunity. More recently you had Farranferris, which was a possibility for both UCC and CIT, but no go.'

When the city was suffering in the 1980s, how aware was UCC? To what extent did the thousands of job losses resonate in academia? Former UCC President Gerry Wrixon considers the question.

'I have to say I don't think it resonated. There was no connection. Jobs there – in UCC – were and probably are a bit too secure, and in any case the salaries were being paid from Dublin. The connection between activities at a local level and the pay packet you got at the end of the month – that connection was not made. I think so, anyway. That was the impression I had.'

Wrixon could compare the Cork university with other, more engaged institutions elsewhere.

'I certainly thought it was more remote back then, but it was the way the world was going. I'd been in the States for eleven years and I'd seen the input local universities had into their cities, into the growth of industry – without compromising their academic standards.

'But UCC … it was a small university dominated by the arts and humanities. Their natural inclination would have been to shy away from this kind of thing – not that they would have been against it, necessarily, but engineering was a small part of it.

'In fairness, the department of chemistry would have been close to the chemical plants going up in Cork, so it had happened to a certain extent in that department. But I think the NMRC probably had a more lasting impact.'

14

Blood on the Carpet: Haughey Helps Cork

Cork's eventual status as a hi-tech hub and centre of the knowledge economy was not inevitable. Turning into the 1980s two obvious drivers of the city's technological reputation, with concomitant benefits for industry and employment, were UCC and Cork RTC, the third-level institutions of learning.

However, the latter was not yet a decade in existence, and UCC, as noted, often seemed remote from the city's concerns. Furthermore, in a college dominated by arts and humanities faculties, how could an area like electronics carve out its own identity?

Gerry Wrixon stumbled across the news report late in the 1970s, and the electrical engineering lecturer could see the opportunity between the lines.

'What happened was that Ireland lost out to Scotland on a particular industry or factory being located here because there was a microelectronics centre in the University of Edinburgh, which was an attractive proposition to industry. I remember reading in the paper Dessie O'Malley saying that if we needed a national microelectronics centre then we should have one in Ireland.

'The National Board for Science and Technology was given a brief to look at all the options and to come up with a plan for such a centre, and needless to say, it came up with a plan to have it built in Dublin.'

Wrixon was, at that point, the only person in Ireland working in this particular area, 'in universities anyway'. Before he left Bell Labs in the US to come back to UCC, one of his specialities was working with a particular kind of semiconductor device.

'I knew it was in demand in Europe, so before I came here, to make sure I had something to work with, I arranged for a laboratory to be set up, funded by the Germans, French and English, a European laboratory which was a precursor of the NMRC. We were building this up and nobody else in an Irish university was doing this type of work, so when I read this proposal to put a microelectronics centre in Dublin I felt it didn't make sense.'

Then Wrixon's connection to a certain politician came into play. He'd installed those solar cells on that Kerry island, hadn't he?

'I rang Charlie Haughey and told him it didn't make sense, so he said to come up and see him. I was in Dublin soon after and I rang, but he was very busy. "How are you getting back to Cork," he asked me, and I was flying back, so he offered me a lift to the airport because he would be going home that way. So the meeting was in his car.

'We sat into the car and discussed it: he told me "everybody agrees you should be in charge of it, but that it has to be in Dublin, because it's the biggest city," and so on. I said, "If that's the reason then none of us should live anywhere else, that doesn't make sense at all. And anyway, you can't order this off the shelf. It has to be an organic outgrowth of an existing facility. You build on that." He said he'd think about it.'

Wrixon got out of the car and Haughey sped off.

It is worth pointing out that at that stage the plan for the centre was more than a possibility for Limerick: it was being firmed up, with the key players already notified of the impending decision and making the necessary arrangements. Wrixon himself saw the evidence first-hand.

'It's interesting the way things work out. At the time Dessie O'Malley was the minister responsible for industry, and a former classmate of mine, Ed Walsh, was in the University of Limerick. While the location of the centre was being discussed, Ed rang me up: "Gerry, this centre – O'Malley was on to me and said it'll either be built in Dublin or Limerick; why don't you move up here to Limerick and bring all your people, we'll build the centre here on the campus?"

'I said, much as I'd said to Haughey, "I don't want to move – we have an ideal location here."

'He was saying it would either be Dublin or Limerick, so I rang Haughey again: "What's all this nonsense? The place for this is Cork, and Cork needs something like this." Apple was starting off, there was an opportunity here.'

Namechecking Apple is significant. Wrixon points out that it was not a case of simply feeding graduates from a microelectronics centre into the factory in Hollyhill: the centre's purpose was more nuanced than that.

'We weren't exactly doing what Apple were doing, but a lot of this was education as well. You've got to be researching, educating, developing all the time.

'It was the people who were attractive at the end of the day, because they were what was ultimately attractive to industry, they could work in the different industries coming to Cork. And they could and did spawn different industries – our closest people that we worked with were initially Analog Devices in Limerick, but now the whole place is filled, top to bottom, with ex-NMRC graduates. It all worked out very well.'

Not least for UCC. Though the NMRC had a campus which was far more restricted in terms of access than the grounds of UCC itself, it was more visible than the college, located as it was on the river near the Mercy Hospital.

There was a separation of identity between UCC and the NMRC but a link persisted nevertheless in the public mind, to UCC's benefit. In that context the NMRC's close links to industry served to give UCC an associated boost in reputation, particularly in terms of perceived detachment from the city's travails throughout the 1980s.

Wrixon's original interest in links between third-level education and industry had been one of the driving forces in the separation of the two institutions.

'Exactly. That was one of the reasons I was so anxious the NMRC had a separate identity to UCC. At the time, universities had a reputation for not being that interested in the problems of industry, or of the outside world generally. I wanted to make sure when we went to industry and said, "look, we can solve your problem" that we had our own way of doing so, that I had an industry background, all of that.'

There was an ironic side to the NMRC's location, then – it was based in the Maltings, a site on the north channel of the Lee, owned by UCC but which had originally been home to a large industrial enterprise as far back as the eighteenth century. Flour mills, a brewery – the River Lee Porter Brewery – and a malting operation had all operated on the site. In the early years of the nineteenth century Beamish and Crawford had taken over the River Lee Porter Brewery. When the NMRC opened in 1982, then, it was a case of cutting-edge technology coming back to the site, a mere two centuries after it had begun there.

That NMRC opening provided Wrixon with a few headaches ahead of time. For one thing, Haughey, who had been the moving force in locating the centre in Cork, was no longer in power, but he would still have to be invited. For another, the current Minister for Energy would have to come. Would there be an atmosphere?

'John Bruton was the minister responsible,' says Wrixon. 'The government had changed by the time it was opened and Haughey was leader of the opposition. We were still in touch and I got on to him, saying, "look, it's being opened," and he said, "well, I should be at that." I told him it was being opened by Bruton and he said, "Okay, that'll be all right, I know him well enough."

'We'd invited Hugh Coveney as well, but as it turned out he couldn't come. On the day itself I went out and met Bruton in front of the building, and there in front of us was Haughey. On one side he had another Cork TD Gene Fitzgerald, and on the other side more Fianna Fáil politicians, all of them laughing at a joke or a story Haughey was telling, and Bruton turned to me: "Excuse me, Professor Wrixon, but did you invite anybody of my political persuasion?"

'And I had, they just hadn't shown up.'

After a brief ceremony, Wrixon brought the guests on the traditional tour of the laboratories and classrooms.

'We went through the facility, and one thing that impressed me happened when we took the VIPs on a tour of the centre. We had half a dozen different laboratories – computer-aided design, fabrication, the whole lot – and in each of them I had the group leader in that lab explain to the visitors what was going on. In simple terms, just an overview of their work. In each of them Haughey asked an intelligent question: in other words, he listened to what he was being told, absorbed it and responded. Bruton and the others kept their mouths shut.

'Bruton was called away for a phone call and came back to us for lunch. When we sat down Haughey said, "You had to take a phone call there, John?"

'Bruton said, 'Don't worry about it, Charlie, just a crisis in Dublin I had to solve."

"'Nothing too minor, I hope," Haughey said.'

Wrixon is frank about the timing of the opening. They were ahead of the curve. Just about.

'In terms of the activities of the centre, we were lucky in that it came into being right when the EU was starting its framework research programmes. Now they're on framework 12, but we were there at the very beginning, which was good for a number of reasons. First, you wouldn't be allowed in unless your work was up to a high standard. There was no reinventing the microelectronic wheel here in Cork – if we were going to be involved with European partners, then we had to deliver.

'In terms of contacts and keeping our standards up, that was invaluable, but it also meant we got lots of funding. We got state funding for the capital equipment, so we were educating people, developing contacts with industry such as Analog Devices, Apple, EMC, General Semiconductor out in Macroom, and we had a lot of computer-aided design companies which started up, and we were integrated with them.

'It was slow but it happened. A lot of these high-added-value industries don't happen until the people are there to actually do the work. You can't have computer-aided design companies come in somewhere unless there are people there who can do computer-aided design, obviously.

'It all worked in tandem – you worked with industry and educated the kids, they get their master's or PhD, they go off and get some experience and come back … That's the way it's happened ever since, through the transition to the Tyndall Institute.'

The NMRC is no longer, of course. Since 2004 it has been known as the Tyndall Institute, thanks to the then-President of UCC.

'That was a rebranding exercise,' says Wrixon. 'I was President of UCC then and we were going to expand the centre, we were looking for big investment to modernise the equipment and to revamp more of the Maltings, the old college building where it was based, and to bring in more people from other UCC departments.

'It was just electrical engineering originally, but we wanted to bring in physics and biology and chemistry – we wanted to bring in people from the Institute of Technology, because they had a big group of people in the opto-electronic field in particular. Through Science Foundation Ireland a big group came in from England, there was a new director appointed, so there was so much change happening that they wanted to rebrand it, and it was ideal to do that all together.'

It was also ideal in terms of attracting industry to the area. Wrixon points out that having an internationally-recognised hi-tech research centre in Cork helps the Industrial Development Authority (IDA) in its work, for instance.

'I think it was good for Cork reputationally, absolutely. It's just one string to the bow, but if you don't have that bow … it means there's a core of people here, highly educated in this area – though it's broadened out considerably – and they're available to join start-ups, to start start-ups. It's a resource. It gives confidence to the IDA, which uses it all the time, and it gives people the confidence to know they can work at the highest level.'

When still lecturing in electrical engineering in UCC, Wrixon also got those working in the NMRC to contribute to that faculty, to the benefit of both institutions.

'I lectured in the electrical engineering building and went down to the NMRC then as well. The students had to do a final-year project down there – if they were interested in electronics they came down there to the NMRC.

'I also persuaded a lot of the people we hired there, in the NMRC, that it would look good on their CVs if they taught a course in the electrical engineering department. We didn't charge the department for that, but we still brought in a whole new range of courses in microelectronics by doing so, a range they didn't have before that and which didn't cost it anything.

'There's a thing in Ireland that you're either a researcher or a teacher when you're in academia, but to me I always felt you had to mix the two. And we did.'

Wrixon's long service in the college means he can compare the eighties and the noughties when it comes to evaluating how integrated UCC is into the life of the city.

'I think it's more integrated now. Definitely. Those departments which can be relevant to the development of Cork can be relevant, and much more so than they used to be.

'Whether or not UCC is as integrated into Cork as NUIG seems to be in Galway, I would doubt. Even now, when I go to events, concerts or whatever, you see very few people from UCC there. Maybe I don't know them any more. Obviously integration depends a lot on the individual faculty member, and how much they want to get involved in the city. And many of them are not from Cork, they maybe find it difficult to involve themselves.'

There's still room for expansion, of course. Wrixon points out the diversity of interests in the Tyndall, but there are other areas into which UCC can expand, and not on its own, either.

'In the microelectronics area, the Tyndall has metamorphosed into different things. There's a probiotic centre run by Fergus Shanahan which is quite successful. It employs a couple of hundred people, has good links with industry ... There's a lot of software development going on in UCC, and I was very impressed with a visit to the National Software Centre. That's backed by both UCC and CIT [Cork Institute of Technology] – I think there needs to be some development or research work going on, educating people to a reasonably high level to help them start their own companies or to join or attract a multinational here.

'There's a lot going on between the university and CIT, more than people realise. They're embedded in the Tyndall and UCC and CIT do a joint degree in architecture, while there's also a biomedical or bioscience degree which they do together. There's a lot more that could be done. In engineering, my own field, CIT has civil engineering, mechanical engineering, electrical engineering – and we have the exact same in UCC. That's a waste of taxpayers' money, in my opinion. Duplication.

'Those courses could be rationalised. The diploma and technician courses in CIT? They could be done jointly; there's a certain amount of rationalisation which should go on – but that's the problem with Ireland, isn't it? There's no local input. What looks like happening with CIT is that they're going to go in with IT Tralee, which doesn't make any sense whatsoever.

'We should be trying to build up our local area here, and to rationalise that – but there's no incentive to do that. All the diktats come from Dublin. If there were more evidence of collaboration or rationalisation ... it's the same with adult education, where UCC and CIT both run a bunch of courses. Surely that could be rationalised or co-ordinated in some way.'

As a footnote, years after the NMRC was opened, Wrixon happened to be in Dublin at a time when Haughey was back as Taoiseach. The academic rang the politician and was invited to see the Department of the Taoiseach's spanking-new offices.

'That was the "Chas Mahal", I visited him there, and he asked if I wanted to see the cabinet room. In we went, and he showed me the cabinet table – which was made in Kilbrittain, incidentally – and as he went around the room he said, "I sit here, this minister sits here, that minister sits there, and that's where all the blood was shed for your effing microelectronics centre."

'"Oh dear," I said, "was there a lot of trouble about that?"

'"There was," he said, "only myself and Gene Fitz against the rest of them."

'"God, I'm very sorry about that, Taoiseach," I said.

'"Don't worry about it, Gerry," he said. "Nothing I couldn't handle."'

15

'A Place for Women'

Looking back now, it was a cruel decade for women, and not just in Cork. At a national level there were heartbreaking stories such as that of Ann Lovett, the fifteen-year-old who died after giving birth, alone, in a Longford grotto in January 1984.

Later that same year the Joanne Hayes case became headline news for weeks on end. The Kerrywoman signed a confession to the effect that she had killed her baby and flung it into the sea, the body eventually washing up on a beach near Cahersiveen.

Hayes had had a baby on the family farm, which had died at birth – 50 miles north of Cahersiveen – and her blood type did not match that of the baby found on the beach. Nevertheless, she was charged with murder, with gardaí floating a bizarre theory of superfecundation – that she had been impregnated by two different men.

In October 1984 the charges were dropped and in January the following year a tribunal of inquiry opened into how those charges had been brought.

This tribunal soon became a matter of investigating Joanne Hayes and her conduct – she was cross-examined for five days and faced 2,000 questions, many of them searching inquiries about her private life.

At another level the entire country was coming to grips with legislation and morality. In October 1983, there was a bitterly divisive referendum to give constitutional recognition to the equal right to life of the unborn and the mother – the eighth amendment.

At one public meeting on the matter an opponent of the amendment was described by a speaker as having 'the morals of a tomcat', which would have been one of the kinder epithets slung around. The amendment passed comfortably.

Three years later it was proposed to remove the constitutional ban on divorce, the referendum on the tenth amendment, but those in favour of retaining the ban took a different tack in this campaign, triggering fears about succession and property rights. The amendment was defeated.

In retrospect, the two votes could be seen as the last great flick of the Church's whip in Irish politics: hence the famous comment by an anonymous voter that the hierarchy had won the day with a Carmelite in one hand and the ballot box in another. The humour struck home precisely because it was true.

Cork was no oasis of feminism in the country at that time; in fact, it was of a piece with the rest of Ireland. Kathleen Lynch campaigned in the two referendum campaigns mentioned and can give nuance to the role of the Church, then and now, in the country.

'I've never been anti-Church. We don't have a properly developed civic system in this country, a sense of civic responsibility, because we handed that over to the Church – they didn't ask for that, by the way, we handed it over – but if you don't have that you need something to show people what's right, what's wrong.

'My mother used to say to us, "will I have to write that down for you?"; she knew that we knew right from wrong.

'We abdicated that responsibility to the Church, and the Church has a right to be listened to. There's a difference between listened and influenced, though, and the state has the responsibility of rebutting the Church's arguments if they don't benefit the people.

'In that first divorce referendum it was a matter of recognising reality, but we couldn't get that across. The counter-message, "hello divorce, goodbye Daddy", was very strong, even though there were plenty of cases where Daddy was gone anyway. But the fear that was caused was huge. It wasn't a rational argument, it was fear, pure and simple. That kind of fervour drove people to Ballinspittle as well.

'By contrast, with the marriage referendum a few years ago, when we were advising groups we told them it would be won by people's grannies. If they wanted their grandchildren to marry the people they loved, they'd win the referendum.'

It was very different in the 1980s. Take the 1983 referendum on abortion, when fear was the key.

'The abuse we got from people portraying themselves as super-Christians, super-Catholics ...' says Lynch. 'We opposed it on the basis that it would cause huge difficulties afterwards, and it has. There were significant people who voted to keep it out, but the fervour, the fear ... it was easy to frighten people.

'I was read from the altar, yeah. The priest giving out about me, all of that. The same in the divorce referendum a few years later, when you'd hear "just because you want to get rid of your husband." I remember during that referendum a woman saying to me, "Kathleen, what about the land?" The same woman – who I'd have regarded as sensible – was living in a corporation house. Literally. "How much do you have?" I asked her.

'But that approach, putting fear into people, that worked. We're thirty years on and that has changed dramatically. I wouldn't be saying everything is fantastic now, and when it comes to abortion I would have opinions on certain issues – but that's just my opinion, I wouldn't force it down your throat. You've no idea of what you'd hear on the doorsteps from people. Venom. Your kids being told, "do you know your Mammy wants to ...", and they'd be saying, "What, my Mammy loves babies." It was horrendous.'

Away from the *Sturm und Drang* of the constitutional battles, women faced other battles, though Ronnie Dorney, a social worker through the decade, makes a valid case for context when looking at the 1980s.

'As time goes on awareness rises, generally. If you look at any particular time, then everything is acceptable. I had a grandmother who was twenty-three in 1916, so she didn't have the vote then – she had no property, nor did my grandfather.

'But people thought that was okay then – rich and poor, that was the way it was. Looking back now we'd think, "how did you put up with that?" Back in the 1980s there were places where women looked after other women who might have been beaten by a man. It was deemed to be okay to hit your wife, then, but because we change and evolve over time, we now see that as totally unacceptable.

'But again, that's hindsight. You're retrofitting your views on a time when – for instance – you couldn't get a loan without your

husband co-signing for it. And that was deemed okay because …
that was the way it was.

'There was a place for women. There was some support for
women who were victims of domestic violence, but it was also a
time, don't forget, when it was okay to strike children in school.

'When I went to school if you went home and said "the teacher
slapped me", my parents' reaction was "what did you do?" That
has changed totally and slapping is completely unacceptable. So
our views changed totally in that regard, but nowadays we'd be
totally surprised that that even happened back then, that it was
allowed to happen.'

The role of women in disadvantaged areas in the 1980s was
crucial, says Dorney: 'They were holding families together, which
is often a woman's role. If someone called to the door they went
out to speak to them.'

There was female representation on Cork City Council in
1985 as Kathleen Lynch explains: 'Everyone's experience was
different, but regarding the institutional image of women, which
was the message to the Irish population, there were only three
women elected to the Corporation in 1985, for the second half of
the Cork 800.

'You had Chrissie Aherne of Fianna Fáil, who was widowed
with her family reared, at one end of the spectrum. She'd been
quite a successful public representative for quite a few years and
brought her view of the world. You had Mairin Quill, who was
unmarried, professional – a schoolteacher – and then you had
me. Young, married with four young children. 'The significant
thing, though, is there were only three of us out of thirty-one.
And we were an oddity.'

As Lynch says, there was an unthinking, unconscious sexism
prevalent in the institutions of the time, though sometimes it
wasn't that unconscious.

'The one thing that you'd have run into at that time is men saying, "who's at home minding your children?",' she says. 'I got that a lot. I would have done a lot of social welfare appeals – successfully, I'd have to say – but if there were cases of women in employment out sick, the one question that would be asked in the interview with a deciding officer was very often, "and who'll mind your children?"

'I won more appeals on that question than anything else. All you had to say was "I went in with a man for an appeal last Monday but you never asked him that question". That's why that came into the Equal Status Act, those kinds of argument.'

As a politician Lynch found she had to convince women as well as men that she – and they – could participate.

'Women would ask me how I did it, saying they couldn't imagine being there to get the kids out to school, there again for lunch, and do all the work in between.

'But now women take that as just something that has to be done. You organise yourself. You're not expected to do as much, though women still do more.

'When women said that to me, though, "I couldn't imagine doing all that," I always said, "well, do you think you could do what he does", referring to a man they knew, and they'd say, "ah yeah." Then I'd say, "what's the difference?"'

There was often ignorance behind the sexism, she adds: 'First we were an oddity, and such a mixed bunch, so different; and second, I think some of them would have been less inclined to take me on compared to someone who wouldn't have been as quick to bite back.

'Ironically, it was much later than the 1980s when I really took offence at a comment made in the chamber by someone who should have known a lot better, someone who apologised afterwards.

'But you got casual, unthinking sexism from the public. "If I was your husband" was a big one, and my response to that was always "If you were, you'd be counting your lucky stars." That was common. As was the assumption you weren't married at all, that that was the only reason you could do the job.

'It was uninformed, and I wouldn't take offence with a comment from someone who's uninformed, because it's your job to inform them. But that's the way it was.'

Making a difference to women's lives even at a local level could be a challenge, says Lynch. She found she had to come at some issues obliquely.

'I learned very early on that you could approach local politics in a very direct, straightforward way, the way men had always done, if you wanted – but the decisions men were going to make had been made anyway, so you had to do it a little differently as a woman. For instance, I had a double buggy at the time, our last two kids had only a year between them. Getting up and down footpaths wasn't just a nightmare with it, it was downright dangerous, because you were left out on the road exposed to traffic. I wanted the footpaths that were dished, which is now the norm, something very straightforward and which was needed – generally you had bigger families in the 1980s, don't forget.

'But that couldn't happen, and there was a sense of "what on earth would women want that for?" I was thinking, "right, how do I get around this?" – so I decided to put down a motion on wheelchair access.

'And that was fine. The first footpath dished was the one outside Dunnes Stores in Patrick Street, and while it might not sound like much, it was all about access. If you were trying to get a pram or buggy in or out of Dunnes at that time you knew all about it. The same if you were in a wheelchair or if you were an elderly person.

'Access was the key thing, and women were making those arguments, arguments men didn't make. I didn't blame men for not making those arguments because certainly in the 1980s you didn't see men pushing buggies.

'Thinking like that wasn't part of their lives, and that was fine – that's always been my approach to feminism and men. How can you expect to understand the experience if you haven't had that experience yourself?

'People like Chrissie and Mairin would have had a similar view, I think.'

The struggle for communities that were more marginalised again could be even more acute in the 1980s. Ronnie Dorney can speak from personal experience.

'I was coming out that time and if you mentioned that ... I don't know if you'd even have gotten a job. I was working on a lesbian helpline and an AIDS one, I was doing a lot of work in that area but I wouldn't have put that on a CV.

'It was a bit like the feeling some people had that time about giving an address in some parts of the north side of the city if applying for a job. I used an address of an aunt of mine in Blackrock myself. Even though you might think working on those helplines and so on would have helped my CV, I wouldn't have put them down. I was out to certain people, say, but not in every work situation, put it like that.'

Towards the end of the decade, Dorney went to work in a project on a sixteen-week contract, and towards the end of that period she was called into the office to see the person running the project.

'I thought I was being left go, given it was near the end of the sixteen weeks, and a colleague came along. What had happened was that a letter had been sent to the project about me.

'I went down to the office and the person said, "I have a letter here about you, that you're a known lesbian, and so therefore should not be working with children."

'Nowadays you'd wonder if you had a case against them, but at the time it was one of my most challenging personal experiences. I fluffed them a bit, I said "I'm terribly shocked" and so on, but really I don't know how I got back out of the office to where my colleague was; she'd driven me down, and in fairness, she was so supportive. The only legislation in place was the Incitement to Hatred Act, but even so, it was an anonymous letter, all of that.'

That was a Friday. Dorney says she spent the entire weekend wondering what to do.

'I had a mortgage to pay and didn't want to lose my job, but when you're confronted by something like that you don't want to deny yourself, but at the same time it gave me the resolution that my mental health was more important than a job.

'The reality was that a lot of people lived closeted lives. They had to. Cork is a funny size in that it's small enough. Some people who knew me knew, but there weren't any protections in terms of employment.

'And that's why it was so significant to me in that I said I'd be true to myself – accept me or not, but I wouldn't be put in that kind of position again.'

She remembers the gay community as emerging at that time, even if the range of outlets was limited.

'I remember going with a pal to one bar that used to be on MacCurtain Street – you had to knock on the door to be allowed in – and thinking, "God, this is miserable, I can see why you'd be so down in yourself."

'It was so hidden. You had to know someone who'd get you in and so on. Then Loafers opened, which was great because it was like a community hub, and the Quay Co-op was great also.

'I remember the first Cork Pride march: there were only twenty people who took part in it. People spat at them, made remarks, and I remember Kathleen Lynch saying to Arthur Leahy, "If we don't march, where will the gang coming behind us go?"

'That was the context. People had codes by which they lived, because they had to. The change has been huge: I was chatting to a teenager who came out recently and I said there was an LGBTQ society in UCC. He said, "what would I want to go to that for?", as if it wasn't necessary. Which is great.'

Dorney is correct about the amount of change. Almost a decade after the divorce referendum of 1986, another referendum was passed, giving Irish people the right to divorce. The speaker with 'the morals of a tomcat' in 1983 was President of Ireland seven years later.

And in 2018, the gardaí and the Taoiseach apologised to Joanne Hayes, as science had categorically proved she could not have been the mother of the Cahersiveen baby. Progress of a sort.

16

Going Without

The obvious question to ask is whether the 1980s could have been as bad as we remember. The answer is an unambiguous yes. Going by the bald facts, the evidence is damning. Manufacturing jobs fell by over 25 per cent during the 1980s, with Barry Brunt of UCC's Department of Geography dredging up some unappealing statistics:

> The 1980s was a decade of economic depression for the GCA [Greater Cork Area] and saw manufacturing employment fall by 5,600 [26.5 per cent] ... the first half of the 1980s was particularly difficult with closures and contractions removing over 5,400 jobs from the area's economy. In contrast, new openings and expansions provided only 1,269 jobs ... the identification of Cork city as one of Ireland's unemployment black spots.

Cork's dependence upon declining sectors such as textiles, clothing and footwear, food and drink, defined the severity of the recession.

In 1986 unemployment in the city stood at 23 per cent, but that did not tell the story of how suddenly the dole queues had lengthened. The live register of unemployment for the Greater Cork Area increased by 243 per cent in the four years up to 1984. For instance, in March that year there were 15,583 unemployed people within the city.

Within those figures lurked pockets of even worse deprivation. The 1986 census revealed that 40 per cent of the labour force in Gurranabraher was unemployed; a study conducted in Mayfield showed that in one estate, Roseville, unemployment ran at 60 to 70 per cent, three times the city average. (As a comparison, during the crash following the Celtic Tiger, when the country was regarded as being on its knees, unemployment peaked nationally at 12 per cent in 2012).

Deprivation was very real for those working on the ground. Ronnie Dorney was a social worker in the 1980s and saw what poverty meant.

'I was working part-time in projects across the north side, in Togher, to help youngsters who had huge problems. It was my first experience of a recession. Before that when things were bad, people headed for London. Even if they went without qualifications, they still went, and they found a way.

'I'd have worked with women, for instance, who were trying to manage with very little money. Moneylenders calling to their doors for money, for instance. You'd hear people giving out about those women smoking, for example, when a lot of the time they were smoking to keep hunger pangs at bay. They'd feed the children but have to go without themselves. These were families that were hungry. Literally. The kids we were working with, some of them would have had one pair of shoes; if you were bringing them away on an outing it could be a problem because they only had that one pair of shoes.

'There were youngsters who had the best parents in the world, then, but they'd have a lean time. They had so little money that they could cover the basics, but an event, or some bad luck – if the television broke or there was a First Holy Communion, things that came up might put them really at a huge disadvantage.'

Dorney drifted into social work: 'We had positive role models at school, so that would probably have been the ideal, but to get a job as a teacher … what it was, in the 1980s there was no work. A lot of the people I hung around with emigrated.

'I got subbing work but there were no jobs – you'd get a week's sub, two weeks' sub, but I did a lot of training to upskill myself. In doing that I was probably getting to deal with all the kids who were difficult to engage with. Maybe because I was the new teacher in these places, I don't know. This would have been 1983 to 1987, say. I remember teaching one particular class, what was called social health, and the head said to me afterwards that he could hear a pin drop, and I felt I was just talking to them. I enjoyed the teaching but I also enjoyed talking to people, finding out about them, and with all of that I drifted into youth work.

'The old VEC was developing youth provision, using what used to be youth clubs. On a Monday night I'd be a youth leader in the youth club; I was volunteering in summer schemes, all of that kind of community activity.

'I was wondering what I really wanted to do, and I felt if I was going to engage in it I needed a qualification. The skills of teaching were useful in what I was doing with kids, and I said to myself, "I really enjoy this". So I decided to go back to UCC to train in social work.'

When she left college she found real deprivation in Cork.

'Poverty changes. Don't forget that. What was deemed poor now is different to what was deemed poor then.

'Moneylending was a regular way to get money in the 1980s, for instance. There were credit unions in the city which were terrific to people at that time, absolutely, but you still had to save for ten weeks to establish yourself as a good credit union member, and some people couldn't do that.

'It was the extra cost, the unforeseen thing that happened that put people under pressure immediately. They got enough from social welfare in order to survive, but something out of the ordinary routine would upset everything in terms of money in the family. And if they couldn't go to a credit union, the first port of call was a moneylender. When women collected money from the post office, the moneylender would have the children's allowance book outside the post office – he'd give them the book, they'd collect the money and come outside and hand money, book, everything back.

'They were trying to repay loans with 100 or 200 per cent interest, so in real terms they had no chance of paying them off. The likes of MABS [the Money Advice and Budgeting Service] was developed in the 1980s because moneylending was so prevalent.

'We were working with people in debt to moneylenders for that classic reason – something came up that they couldn't pay for and the moneylender got their hooks into them then.'

Kathleen Lynch teases the point out further.

'It's like the sales. You never see poor people at the sales because there's no accumulated wealth. But at the time there were no additional luxuries. There was a budget and you couldn't deviate from that. Anything additional … that couldn't be paid for. That impacted on education. People talk now about third-level access.

That was a time you were trying to get them to Leaving Cert., and that was difficult with the cost of books, even uniforms, shoes, the fees for exams. It wasn't that people didn't budget for those. People couldn't.'

Enter the moneylender. But Lynch points out an unpalatable truth: what was the alternative?

'I think people knew exactly what was going on. And for a lot of people it was part of the budget. This is going to sound awful, but you have to remember that until credit unions came along – more specifically, until they became embedded in communities, because they were around from the 1960s onwards – what bank would give you a loan?

'Even if it was only a hundred pounds, and you were diligent and could pay it back, they wouldn't entertain you.

'It's not as if people weren't aware of the banks. They were. They weren't stupid – but they also knew that approaching the banks for money was a waste of time, pure and simple.

'I know the moneylenders fleeced people, but they were also the only source of instant additional finance in a time of crisis. You'd hear people talk about parasites and so on, but where were the banks then? You see what has emerged regarding the banks in recent years, and you'd have to ask: who were the parasites there?

'On top of that, if you were a woman dealing with money in the house, which was often the way, you had another dynamic again. I'd be the tougher of the two of us in dealing with a bank, say, for a loan to cover election expenses. But my husband had to come with me if we were getting that loan. Granted, it was his name if the loan went wrong – I was getting the money on his name – but at that time your husband had to go with you for the loan. And women were generally the household managers, which made it even more ridiculous.

145

'I think it was only when women took senior posts in the banks that that changed. They recognised who to deal with if they had a husband and wife sitting across from them.'

The chances of an unemployed couple making it as far as an interview with the bank in the 1980s were pretty slim, as Lynch points out.

'I go back to people not being able to afford to send their kids to school. In a household where that was true, you had nobody getting up for work in the morning because they had no work to go to. Because of that the kids could be up late, and stay out late, roaming around – and, in some cases, joyriding.

'The unemployment had an effect on the social structure. If the wage earner lost their job they lost the structure to their day, and that could spread through the entire house. I remember making appointments for people and a friend warned me about that. "Don't be surprised if you make an appointment for someone to be somewhere for noon on a Tuesday and they don't show up, because some people have no structure to their lives when it comes to the days of the week."

'That happened to me, I'd make appointments and people wouldn't turn up. My mother used to joke that only for Sunday we wouldn't know what day of the week it was, but in some cases that was truer than you realised.'

Ronnie Dorney says there were chinks of light in the darkness, for all that.

'Some of the kids I worked with are long gone – suicide, drugs, all of that. It would have been the lucky ones who got away. There was a grimness in the city, certainly. Poverty. But I also saw people helping each other, real neighbourliness, real resilience. And that can be underestimated. I saw a lot of happiness in families.

'There can be a sense of people only wanting to see the bad, viewing things through the lens of a professional – "isn't that terrible?" But I saw kids who were very happy as well. There was a lack of opportunities for young men in particular, compared to the noughties when young men in similar situations were able to get jobs and rear families.

'In any recession the first people to be hit are always the poorest, so they're the first people to lose their jobs, while there's a significant cohort of people in this country who made a lot of money out of the last recession.

'There's an infrastructure in place now that wasn't there in the 1980s. The economics of the time put pressure on people, on relationships, and the sadness of what that did to families was clear – but families were able to function and be happy, too. Kindness and warmth were what I saw, people supporting each other. Often you'd wonder how other people, in similar circumstances, would have dealt with the same pressures.'

And some parts of the city saw more of those pressures than others.

17

The North Side

When Cork settled down to work on the main drainage scheme some years ago, one part of the plan in particular attracted a lot of attention: the location of the treatment plant.

There were plenty of sites discussed, evaluated, inspected and dismissed before the decision was eventually made, and Little Island was selected.

The choice was not made before lengthy debates about the process in the City Council, with councillors speaking at length about how unsuitable certain sites were due to highly technical reasons, usually their closeness to the constituency of the councillor who was speaking. The late Dave McCarthy, who represented the Knocknaheeny area for many years, was at one of these debates, and reportedly said: 'I don't know what all the fuss is about. I only know that if this stuff could flow uphill the plant would be put up in Knocknaheeny.'

McCarthy summed up in one sentence a long-simmering attitude in Cork, particularly among those living north of the Lee – that their side of the city had been neglected for years. The 1980s underlined that sense of neglect, principally because of decisions taken years beforehand.

For instance, a quick roll call of significant Cork institutions created in the 1960s and 1970s would include serious, prestigious employers such as the Cork Institute of Technology/Regional Technical College, Cork University Hospital/Regional Hospital, the IDA Technology Park, and the area headquarters of FÁS, the ESB and the Cork Gas Company respectively.

All were located south of the river, providing over 10,000 jobs in those areas, jobs which were largely unaffected by the closures of the 1980s (with the exception of the Cork Gas Company). In contrast, once the 1980s rolled around, the North Infirmary, the only general hospital on the north side of the city, was shut down.

A complicating factor in discussing this division is the vexatious matter of Cork snobbery, a concept too slippery to be simply a matter of geography. Ronnie Dorney, who has worked all over the city, gives a blunt assessment of a subject that could fill volumes: 'It's if you're from the south side – but somewhere like Ballyphehane or Togher – you were a norrie with attitude, while if you were from Montenotte or Sunday's Well … well, that wasn't the north side, really.'

Without large-scale employers such as the institutions mentioned above to take the strain, the Ford and Dunlop closures bit particularly deep north of the river.

'The lesson was not to have all your eggs in one basket,' says Kathleen Lynch. 'To have a city dependent on a couple of major industries like that … it was catastrophic, and more catastrophic for the north side than the south side.'

'I'm not a believer in the north-side-being-done-down narrative but the facts were that on the south side you had more people with trades, and you also had more people in administration. My husband Bernard's aunt worked in Dunlop's, but she worked in the office.

'You had the university, CIT, the hospitals, all of those were on the south side, and it was only natural that people living there or near there would work in those places. 'That's not to say there weren't tradespeople or qualified people on the north side of the city, but in the main not as many of them would have worked for high-profile employers. That was just a fact of life.'

Pat Casey, a reporter with the *Irish Examiner*, draws a parallel between the North Infirmary, Ford and Dunlop.

'There was a burgeoning policy of trying to rationalise hospitals that hadn't been articulated as having "centres of excellence" at the time, but there was probably an echo of Ford and Dunlop in that the hospital was just too small.

'But the north side of the city was impotent in political terms at the time, really. Across a whole range of metrics – education, recreational facilities, political and business influence – the south side was where the action was. I know that sounds trite when it comes to a small European city but there was a significant difference. It took a long time for the north side to find its voice.

'But it was like two cities. All the social housing with the exception of Togher and Ballyphehane in one side of the city, with no facilities for recreation, limited economic activity, and then everyone was surprised there was joy-riding. There was joy-riding because there were no facilities, so it was reaping the whirlwind to a degree.

'The 1980s were transformational across a range of areas, in terms of people finding their voices, finding alternatives, so from that point of view it was a formative time. It was formative on the basis of tough experience, and eventually the city and its inhabitants had to face being another Detroit, if you like, or it would have to get going and help itself.

'I think the latter has pertained, by any yardstick. The change has been immense, and positive, notwithstanding different things that have occurred from time to time.'

Among those different things was state intervention. Sometimes it helped. Sometimes it didn't.

'When people had money in the late 1970s and early 1980s, and mortgage interest relief was introduced, that was very significant. I know people who used that to keep their homes.

'The housing finance agency was introduced – something which wouldn't be a bad idea even now – where people could transfer their mortgage from 18 per cent interest rates to what was, in effect, a state-run bank. That helped them to keep their homes as well.

'The circumstances were exceptional and those were great responses. They worked really well. But there was one thing that happened which didn't work that well, even though it was a measure introduced with the best will in the world.'

On the face of it, an £8,000 grant enabling people to move out of local authority housing seems imaginative, but Lynch says: 'We're still dealing with the after-effects of that, I think. People who were able to move out with the aid of that grant meant they all left local authority housing estates – resulting in ghettoisation, and the problems we're still grappling with.

'The motivation was good. The building industry had collapsed and needed a stimulus, and as a result we avoided a housing crisis then, but the unintended consequence was that a lot of people in those estates who were going to sports clubs, running activities, all of that, left those estates.

'It devastated communities. Those were people who were contributing to the communities, but by definition they also had the wherewithal to leave. So they left.'

The sense of two cities was probably at its sharpest when the North Infirmary closed in 1987. It shocked the entire north side of the city and provoked huge anger; the decision left dwellers north of the river without a hospital apart from the Orthopaedic, a specialist facility at the top of Gurranabraher.

For one politician there were particular associations with the Infirmary. Kathleen Lynch was struck by a bus as a child and had long years of surgery and rehabilitation in the hospital.

'I spent years there and hated the place with a passion, but that wasn't because the people there were cruel or unkind, it was because I spent so much of my childhood in there and had so much pain there. They saved my life, really. They got me walking, and I give the nuns credit for this – though they mightn't want that credit – they let me read. No television, no iPad, no phone. I had a transistor radio which my father had to save for, so I read.

'I tell the nuns they're responsible for my taste in reading. Nothing with sex or romance, no Mills and Boon or *Woman's Way*, but while I was there they left me read Mao Tse Tung and James Connolly, for instance.

'For the majority of people the North Infirmary had been a very good experience there.

'They didn't turn people away, it was spotlessly clean and people didn't get MRSA, put it that way.'

Bernard Allen takes the view that the closure was ultimately self-inflicted.

'I was on the board of management of the hospital, and it was the consultants there who ran the place. There were plenty of warnings given to them – "you'll have to negotiate with the

Mercy Hospital; you'll have to take certain specialities to become expert in, and the same for the Mercy".

'There was to be a role for both hospitals in the division of specialities, but the two sets of consultants couldn't agree. They fought like dogs. When you questioned them about it at board of management meetings you were told, "we know better, we're the consultants". But they couldn't agree. And eventually Barry Desmond, who was Minister for Health, decided to cut the one which was performing worse.'

It suffered because it was well run. He says: 'The ironic thing about the North Infirmary was that it was efficient. When cuts had to be made there was nothing there to cut, and services deteriorated. In other hospitals there was flab, and when cuts had to be made there was something they could get rid of. Not the North Infirmary, so it was closed.

'Because it came after four or five years of closures and financial body blows to the community, a lot of people employed in Ford's and Dunlop's were living on the north side, it was as much psychological as anything else. After everything, you were taking their hospital away.'

It also impacted on Allen's career: 'I was Fine Gael health spokesman at the time and I opposed the Tallaght Strategy [wherein Fine Gael pledged limited support to a minority Fianna Fáil government]. When Alan Dukes announced it a number of us wanted to resign but we were persuaded to stay on.

'So in the Dáil we were going along with Fianna Fáil's proposals, including the closure of the North Infirmary, but locally we were saying it should stay open. The reason it was closing was the regime of cutbacks we were supporting nationally.

'Eventually I got my way on the front bench and at our meeting on this particular Thursday we decided to oppose the Health Estimate the following week.

'There was a regional conference in Limerick that Sunday and there I announced we'd oppose the Health Estimate at Private Members' the following Tuesday and Wednesday in the Dáil; we were supporting the Labour motion opposing the Estimate, and winning that vote would have meant the end of the Tallaght Strategy, and a general election, because it was a financial provision.

'A number of what I'd call the "wets" on the Fine Gael front bench asked for a rethink that Tuesday. They set out the implications of winning the vote, particularly the election – that we might do worse in the election.

'I'd announced it on Sunday, and now this ... I offered Dukes my resignation but he asked me to stay with it, adding that there'd be a reshuffle coming up. I was supposed to become Cork's lord mayor that year anyway, so I did – against my better judgement, it was one of my political mistakes.

'He had his reshuffle, but it was done unexpectedly, and I was lumped in with the rest who were fired, but I'd had to go because I was devoting most of the year to the mayoralty.'

Being squeezed between national obligations and local loyalties took its toll on some.

'There was a contradiction there all the time,' says Allen. 'And you were caught in it. You were defending the closure and voting for it nationally but locally ... I got away with it politically because Fianna Fáil got the blame for it. Denis Lyons, whose seat in the Dáil would have been regarded as safe, lost his seat in the next election because of that.'

'It was a blood-and-bandage station at the end of its days, and the closure was more symbolic than anything else. Did it affect the north side medically or health-wise? No. The Mercy was only across the river.

'The symbolism was everything – "they've stripped us of our jobs, and now they're taking a hospital away from us". It came across as heartless.

'The alternative was for the Minister to call the two teams of consultants in and to tell them they had twelve months to sort it out or one group of them would have to go. In the long term I think it was a good decision because the Mercy was developed, and a lot of good specialities went in there; if I ever got sick I'd go to the Mercy before CUH, to be honest.

'Now they're asset-stripping it, I think. They've been put under the control of the HSE, which controls its capital allocation and makes all the decisions; some of the senior consultants in the Mercy are being told there's no more investment in their speciality, that they have to head out to CUH.

'To me, the long-term strategy is a second major hospital in Cork. Some people want it in Curraheen, others want it in St Stephen's in Glanmire, where there's a huge campus but access is poor, and others want a greenfield site. But that's another day's work.'

For Kathleen Lynch, it was the symbolism of the closure: getting rid of a hospital when, in her words, a hospital was all the north side had.

'It was a catalyst, really. I always maintain that if you want the north side to develop you need a northern ring road – the notion that the road going up Farranree is the northern ring road is beyond me – but regarding the North Infirmary, while I have a jaundiced view of it, at that point it was all we had. That was the difference.

'It wasn't the Mater Private or St Vincent's, but it was all we had. It was also a major employer in the area, don't forget.

'I'd put it like this. In a marriage break-up, and I've dealt with a lot of them, the row is never about the children or the house or the car. It's about a mangy dog you hated but everything gets concentrated on that and you want to hang onto it no matter what.

'The North Infirmary was like that. It provided a service and was all we had. I'd see it as being like the water charges now, the last straw. Industries had gone, people couldn't afford to send their kids to school …

'More could have been done in terms of the consultants, who I think felt the political anger would save the hospital.

'But what was important was saving the hospital. People should have leaned back and taken a wider view, but it closed. The Orthopaedic wasn't the same: it was a speciality hospital.

'Closing the North Infirmary was a catalyst – it made people think, "if this goes, what else could go?"'

Little enough: the grim joke at the time was that there wasn't much left to go.

18

The Local Authority: Soft Tar

Another local institution had its struggles with the downturn. No one is better qualified to comment on what was then Cork Corporation than Brendan O'Callaghan, who joined the local authority in 1952.

'I stayed there for fifty years and five months. I was the longest-serving member there. I don't think anyone will beat that record as they go in later and leave earlier.'

He started as an office boy before becoming a rent collector, but in the 1960s he changed to collecting rates.

'I said I'd have a bash at it. No training, and a lot of arrears, but luckily the area I got was the north-west section – from Falvey's chemist in Coburg Street to Dublin Hill, north of the river.

'I knew practically everybody in the area and everyone paid me in Coburg Street, Leitrim Street, Bridge Street … it got to a stage where my pockets were bulging with money – no cheques, all cash. When I came back in and made my lodgement, Batty Richmond said I'd have to do better than that, but the rest of the week I did Farranree and Gurranabraher, and he said I'd done a wonderful job. I was the rate collector.'

It gave him a unique perspective on the city. For instance, the collapse in the city's industry during the 1980s could not have come at a worse time for Cork Corporation. After the Fianna Fáil landslide in the 1977 general election, domestic rates were abolished: a huge handicap for a municipal authority under pressure.

'That was a big blow, because straight away you were down a pile of money. The government was supposed to make up the difference but it never did. Those were commercial and domestic rates. I remember meeting Pat Kerrigan [a local politician] at a funeral around that time, and he said to me, "Brendan, what in hell is going to happen?"

'"Pat, you're on the inside, I'm on the outside," I said. But I told Jack Lynch I thought it was a big mistake – I said what he should do is bring the rates down by half, or don't allow the Corporation to increase rates for two or three years – but don't do away with them altogether. It's like the water charges now. We don't like paying those charges. We don't like paying income tax, come to that, but with rates, when you take them off it's hard to put them back on again.'

But because the domestic rates had gone, the commercial rates had to make up the shortfall in their place – that's why rates went up so much during the 1980s, it went down along the line. The Corporation had no other recourse. People complained about the commercial rates because they were carrying the can, but the extra money the government had promised to make up that shortfall never materialised.'

It meant rate collectors like O'Callaghan had to improvise. Bespoke arrangements had to be made, because the alternative would have been no rates at all coming in.

'My arrangement was – I wasn't supposed to do it – but if I went in to a business person and they said they were stuck, I'd say, "You tell me when you can afford something; so long as you have the rates paid within the twelve months I don't care how you pay them."

'They didn't like it in the corporation but I said "if ye can do better, go out and do it." That was my argument. I got on well with the business people; you got to know them. The solicitors, for instance, were grand only that their secretaries often had a bit of an attitude; once they heard you themselves they were fine.

'There was a big business in the city at one stage which was doing very well, but the accountant there asked me if there were any other way we'd accept rates, other than in a once-a-year payment. I told him to pay as it suited. He got onto their head office and they were delighted – and they paid away.

'Back in our office they'd be asking, "why are they paying in that way?" and I'd tell them not to worry about it, that I had my own arrangements. They all knew they had to pay their commercial rates. If they wanted to sell the business, after income tax, the rates had to be paid up. It couldn't be passed on otherwise.

'There were probably a few struggling, but if you could make arrangements you got around that. What was the alternative? If you went to court they still owed the money.'

Interestingly, he contrasts attitudes in the 1980s with the outlook during the boom: 'It was harder to collect rates during the Celtic Tiger than it was in the 1980s.

'People were too fond of the money and they didn't want to part with it – collecting it was far harder. It was like someone building a haystack, the higher it goes the better, and the harder it was for them to part with it.

'I remember counting the money from the collections in the church in Blackpool, and we were chatting in the sacristy, and the priest said, "You know, Brendan, the more unemployment that's there, the better the collection." And it's true. When the Tiger was roaming the country it was harder to get money out of people. They were far fonder of money.'

O'Callaghan's experience of the functioning of the Corporation – now Cork City Council – means he can compare eras. Take the outsourcing of corporation jobs, which began in earnest in the 1980s; he compares work done now by the private companies that replaced those corporation employees with the standards of the Corporation in previous decades.

'The greatest mistake was to reduce the maintenance staff in the Corporation and to give out the work to private concerns. For instance, the road surface around the corner from us had to be repaired, and the contractor came along at ten p.m. to do it one evening: unbelievable noise and disruption, but if you saw the condition of the road, it's terrible.

'That was a huge mistake. The Corporation had its own workers, who normally did a good job. Take the street inspector. He went around the city and if your hedge was hanging out over the fence, over the footpath, he was on to you to get that cut. The same if there were flags loose on Patrick Street or wherever – he'd take a note of that and come back and the flags were made by the Corporation in the yard and sent out in the van to replace the loose ones. Where is that now? For years governments and councils have been moving away from having people working to outsourcing the work, and where has that gotten us?

'The difference between then and now was back then the Corporation had its own engineers in charge, their own clerk of works, the best of material went into Corporation houses. They owned the land, too.'

He echoes other contributors in his views on the Corporation's social housing plans: 'The biggest mistake made was the building of houses in Knocknaheeny. They made a hames of that. They had no foresight. They should have looked at Farranree, which was far better planned and where people had much more scope.

'In general the Corporation did as well as it could. They carried on in difficult times and made the best of a bad lot.

'The one fault I could see was that corporations and councils should be out to make a profit, to create a surplus. The attitude I found was that if the Corporation was allocated £2 million, say, then it was "spend that" – because if you didn't spend it all that year you wouldn't get as much allocated the following year.

'I always felt money should be put aside and carried over. Nobody seemed to understand that as opposed to the "spend it or lose it" attitude. The government should have promoted that more, maybe – they should have pushed the idea that "you're independent of us to an extent, so you're responsible for your own money – and for generating a surplus if you can."

'But instead you had the spending. I remember when the financial year ended on 31 March, and one year, in order to spend the entire allocation, the road in Emmet Place was tarred before that date.

'But the tar was so soft it had to be dug up again – what a waste of public money.'

19

The Tide Turns: Apple

Having left Ford in 1975, Dan Byrne settled into AnCo, which was closely allied at the time to the Industrial Development Authority. His engineering background made him ideal for his new role, as a training adviser for engineering companies, and as the IDA was obviously keen to attract such industries to Ireland, he found himself working closely with that body also.

'At that time and as it still does today, the IDA was trying to attract foreign industry to set up their facilities in Ireland, and part of the package offered to these companies involved capital grants, and another part covered training grants. AnCo worked closely with the IDA to offer those training grants to prospective clients.'

From early on he saw a difference in attitudes compared to his old workplace.

'One of the biggest changes in my life was the difference in culture between Ford's and AnCo. In AnCO when you did something positive then somebody praised you. Your boss or manager would say "well done".

'I'd never heard anything like that in Ford's. Nobody ever praised you. The attitude was "that's your job". You might have done a super job but you weren't going to hear it; you had to rely on yourself and believe that you'd done a good job yourself.

'Having joined AnCO, I remember thinking, "I've done nothing significant here but they think I'm great." That was a huge culture shock for me, knowing that people were appreciative of what you were doing. They weren't trying to knock you, unlike Ford's, where it was survival of the fittest.

'After one or two years I was promoted to a senior training adviser role in AnCo – probably the equivalent of a grade nine in Ford's – and part of my responsibility covered all engineering firms doing business in Munster as well as all the Westinghouse investments, which had facilities all over Ireland. That was my introduction to the task of attracting companies, in conjunction with the IDA, to set up facilities in Ireland.'

Still, working in the combative Ford environment had toughened Byrne. When he combined that experience with the lessons learned in AnCo it helped him in challenging times.

'I brought something else with me from AnCo, a lesson I learned from the manager of the Cork Training Centre which was located in the old Douglas Woollen Mills. His name was Tom McCarthy, and he was a senior guy in AnCo and older than me, so he was a lot more experienced. He once said to me, "I've been around a long time, Dan, and I have come to one conclusion. There are very few geniuses in the world and it took me a while to realise that I probably know as much as most."

'That always resonated with me. It helped when I later met the CEO of Westinghouse, a multibillion-dollar company and I was a little overawed by the experience.'

The circumstances of the meeting did not help either. Byrne was delivering bad news.

'I had to tell him some of his people were screwing up the training programme and were putting at risk their eligibility for training grants. That became a high-pressure situation. The word went out that I would not approve the training programme for Westinghouse, who had millions invested in Ireland and that was true.

'Jack Lynch was Taoiseach at the time and this was brought to his attention by Westinghouse, I assume. I received a call from the Taoiseach's office advising me that Westinghouse was an important company for Ireland. I agreed and said I, too, wanted them to be successful but added that I couldn't sign off on taxpayers' money that they hadn't earned.

'The training in Fords prepared me for all that and to deal with that type of pressure. Surviving four and a half years in the Marina prepared me for many things in future life.'

Working more closely with the IDA, Byrne began to focus on attracting companies to Ireland. There were success stories and near misses, and one near miss that might, in retrospect, have been a success of sorts.

'I'd been to a number of European countries working with the IDA to help attract companies to set up in Ireland. I had also been to the east coast of the US, Baltimore and Pittsburgh, for example, doing likewise. There were near misses, certainly, along the way.

'One that nearly got away, and did get away eventually, was Raybestos Manhattan, who located in Ovens. The reaction from some of the Irish press, the focus on asbestosis and so on, before they launched made them wonder whether they should locate here. They thought long and hard but they located eventually here.

'They didn't last very long because the opposition to them was so strong, and I'm not saying that opposition was wrong – as it turned out it was a dangerous place to work and asbestos was proved to be a very serious health hazard.

'That was one example, but I can't honestly think of another company the IDA missed out on. I certainly can't think of any major company that almost located here but which subsequently went elsewhere.

'At that time the IDA had brilliant people – it still does – and whatever country they were based in, they were always trawling and looking for companies which were growing and which were looking to invest in the European market.'

Eventually the trail led to an obscure company in California which, in an age long before the Internet, seemed far more remote than it does even now. Following an introduction by Regis McKenna, Apple was identified by Declan Collins, the IDA man in Silicon Valley, as a company that might fit Ireland in the late 1970s.

'Regis was Apple's Public Relations consultant at that time,' says Byrne, 'He got an honorary doctorate from UCC a couple of years ago, but at the time he was also consulting for the IDA in the Valley. Declan, who was a new recruit to the IDA, was working out of his own apartment in Menlo Park. He was ably assisted in his discussions with Apple by two other more experienced IDA men from their Dublin office, Barney Usher and Brendan Rossiter. This was late 1979, early 1980.

'Very few people in Ireland had heard of Apple. I remember being asked to go and join Declan to convince this company to locate in Ireland and my first thought was, "Apple, have they got something to do with the Beatles?"'

In March 1980 Byrne travelled to California to meet the mysterious Apple.

'This was before Tim Berners-Lee invented the World Wide Web, so there was no Internet at that time. The personal computer market was in its infancy at the time as well, and it was only the intelligentsia were aware of Apple. Obviously, one couldn't easily research and receive information about the company, or the people you were meeting. I was there for a week attending meetings every day with the Apple people.'

On the Friday of that week, there was an announcement at 11 a.m. in the facility for everyone to down tools. Byrne was puzzled but followed along with the rest of the workforce.

'I was wondering what was going on, but all the employees were brought to a local park, much like Fitzgerald's Park in Cork, and they were having pizza and soft drinks and throwing frisbees.

'"What's going on here?' I asked, and was told that because they'd made their monthly quota – it was the last Friday of the month – by eleven a.m. that day, there was a picnic arranged for all employees.

'I was thinking to myself, "Could this work in Cork? No way, they'd all be in the pub. Declan Collins must be mad, recommending that these nutcases come to Ireland." Wow, did I get that wrong!'

It is not an exaggeration to suggest that Apple's choice of Cork as a location for its European factory is one of the most significant decisions made in the history of the city. It was a close-run thing.

'Much has been written about Apple's reasons for locating its European facility in Ireland,' says Byrne. 'I would say the most critical thing was that Cork, in this case, had an advance factory. It was ready for occupation and Apple were in a hurry. They saw that the European market was growing and they were struggling

166

to meet the demands of the US market, not to mention the European market.

'Second, the fact that the work force were young, well educated and English-speaking was very attractive for Apple. The English-speaking element gave Ireland an advantage over Holland.

'The UK had that as well, of course, and these were the two countries which Ireland were competing against to win the Apple project.'

Both Holland and the UK had strong advocates at board level in Apple, but the man who had to sign off on the decision had an inclination towards Ireland.

'In my opinion, the next most critical component of the decision-making process was that one of the key decision makers was a guy called Carl Carlson, an American who had experience of running a factory in Dublin earlier in his career and who had obviously lived there at that time.

'He had had a brilliant experience in dealing with the IDA, with the turnkey solution they offered – many of their competitors were not as well organised, in that regard. As an organisation they deserve huge credit for that. They were well ahead of their time, and the UK subsequently copied their approach. The way they helped new industries in dealing with all aspects of starting up a business in Ireland was a significant differentiator from other countries and gave Ireland a true competitive advantage.

'A number of Carl's team, including a UK ex-pat, continued to lobby for other locations but Carlson overruled them all and selected Cork.

'By the time I arrived in San Francisco, the decision was well along the road. Declan had done all of the heavy lifting of selling Ireland and had set the platform for the decision.

'Declan had already convinced them of the availability of capital grants, while I now had to show how we could help them in terms of training their workforce and providing them with financial assistance to achieve this.

'There was still potential for movement at that stage – still a chance we might lose it to another country – but before I even got there I would say the decision was 80 per cent across the line. I was merely reinforcing their decision that Ireland was the place to go, and by the end of the week we were comfortable that we had them on side.'

Byrne does not claim to have foreseen Apple turning into the global force it did.

'Did I understand and appreciate what Apple was doing? I can't say I was that visionary, and that I saw what Apple would become. No one could have foreseen that. I was as puzzled as anybody. This was the age when Ken Olsen, CEO and founder of DEC had stated in 1977, that "there was no reason for any individual to have a computer in his home". That was the kind of thinking at that time.

'Steve Jobs, on the other hand, had a totally focused, convincing vision that every home would have one of these. I remember him saying that at one of our meetings and thinking to myself, "is he for real?"

'Jobs was a genius, a flawed genius, but a genius, nevertheless.'

At that point Steve Jobs was far more than the visionary designer worshipped by technology aficionados, the genius who would become the subject of Hollywood movies. Byrne first met him when making a presentation to Apple executives: Jobs walked in and put his bare feet on the table as the Corkman made his pitch. The Californian could be otherworldly and unrealistic, to put it mildly, at one point suggesting the entire Cork workforce could be transplanted to the west coast of America.

But behind the figure who became familiar in the twenty-first century presenting a new Apple product on stage at a launch before the world's media, there lay a far more recognisable figure – a hard-nosed salesman who was prepared to traverse the globe to win an order for his firm. His commitment to Cork in this regard was real and tangible. In the case of one sale order the Cork plant pursued aggressively, Jobs proved crucial.

Byrne was working for Apple by then, and his team had worked hard to make an impressive presentation to the client, but Byrne felt the order was slipping away from Apple. He picked up the phone.

'I rang Steve's administrator in California and asked if Steve could come over. The decision had still not been finalised, so Steve agreed to come to Cork to help.

'At this stage, the legend of Steve was growing, certainly. He wasn't at the level he would reach, but everyone was aware of him. I rang the client and asked if he'd like to meet Steve, and he said he'd be delighted.'

At a friendly breakfast meeting with the client Byrne saw Jobs at work, up close and personal.

'I saw Steve put on a performance that was simply genius at work. Firstly, he charmed the client. Birds from the trees stuff, because if Steve wanted to charm you, he really could.

'Then, he went from charming him to threatening him. It wasn't a physical threat, but he said if the client didn't pick Apple he'd end up with an inferior product, one that "would end up in the trashcans all over Ireland," according to Steve. 'The client was stunned. Then Steve offered him a 10 per cent discount.'

Apple won the contract. And Jobs flew back to California, his work done.

'At that time Steve was not involved in the day-to-day operations of the Cork plant,' says Byrne. 'He was vice-chairman of the company and much of his focus was on the development of the Macintosh with his band of pirates in Cupertino.

'However, if there was a sales opportunity in a country that Apple had invested in and it was in danger of being lost, as was the case in Ireland, he used all of his powers of persuasion to rescue it. That was a red rag to a bull for Steve and he could not resist the challenge of fighting for it.'

Not only did Apple become a huge employer, it served as an advertisement for the IDA and Ireland.

'No doubt,' says Byrne. 'In fact, I'd go further and say Apple was used extensively by the IDA as a role model. When I was MD in Apple Cork, I attended many dinners and meetings with the IDA and representatives of companies which were looking at the possibility of coming to Ireland.

'I wasn't just selling Cork, I was selling Ireland, because Apple was seen as such a success – and the IDA leveraged that heavily to get traction with other industries.'

While he was visiting Apple in Cupertino in California in March 1980, the company had offered Byrne a senior position in Cork.

'I didn't take it because I felt I'd be compromised. I was dealing in millions of pounds worth of grants, which was taxpayers' money, and they were offering me a job. If I'd taken it people could have reasonably assumed that this was why they got the grants.

'I agreed to help them with their start-up in Ireland which was part of my job, after all. Alex Wrafter, was the first MD of Apple Cork and I worked closely with him through the start-up phase in terms of hiring and training their new staff. Alex asked me to join Apple, on a number of occasions but I was reluctant to leave what I was doing in AnCO.'

The IDA and AnCo were able to follow up on their promises.

'Remember, we'd gone to Cupertino in March [1980] and the first product rolled off the line that October. This was unheard of in terms of speed of a start-up in Ireland. It was just six months from finalisation of discussions in the US to the first product rolling off the production line in Cork.

'During the Apple Christmas party in December, Alex asked me again about the possibility of me joining the company. I suggested to him that we meet after Christmas and discuss it further. We met during the first week of January and I joined Apple in March 1981 as a lowly training manager. As they say, the rest is history.'

The contrast between Ford in the 1970s and Apple in the 1980s was a sharp one for Byrne.

'A major lesson I received in Ford's – something which sounds negative – was how *not* to treat people. I was determined that if I was ever in a position of authority I'd do the opposite to many of the practices I experienced in Ford's.

'Also, my thoughts while with Apple in March 1980, that the practices in Cupertino would never fly in Cork, were proved to be completely wrong. Apple did successfully bring the culture from California to Cork when it started up here later that year.

'Alex Wrafter, as MD, had lunch every day sitting next to whoever was at the table when he joined it, irrespective of their position. He certainly didn't eat in a separate canteen – there was no such facility; we all ate together.

'Another important lesson was MBWA, which wasn't that well known at the time – it stands for Management By Walking About. Every day, unless Alex was travelling somewhere, he'd walk the factory floor and talk to people, and I did the same when I became MD.

'We had maybe 700 people at that time and I got to know them all. I would talk to them about their kids, where their kids went to school and most importantly how they felt about their jobs in Apple.

'In Ford's, during my time there, that was totally different. If the senior management walked around, you saluted them. Those were two different ends of the spectrum.'

20

The CIA and the Film Festival

There weren't too many beacons of light when it came to Cork's cultural scene come the 1980s. In literature, Frank O'Connor had immortalised the city in his short stories – it was always surprising to think of *New Yorker* readers digesting tales of Leeside snobbery over their coffee in Manhattan – but he'd passed away in 1966. Seán Ó Faoláin was an equally distant figure.

True, Joan Denise Moriarty's Cork Ballet Company ploughed a lonely furrow for almost fifty years, but ballet was a niche interest even within the arts world. When it came to international recognition, there was the Cork Film Festival. And Rory Gallagher.

Gallagher was a vital presence for the city and a focal point all through the 1970s. Though often away on tour, he made a point of returning regularly; his technical virtuosity and soaring reputation were offset by an easy-going and open public persona.

'You know what the most important thing about Gallagher was?' says Theo Dorgan. 'When he'd come home at Christmas and walk down the street.'

'Precisely that: he'd walk down the street. An international figure. I remember lads running across Patrick's Bridge to say hello, and he'd say hello – but they wouldn't bother him. He was let go, because he was at home.'

'There was a pride in not giving him grief, in not hanging out of him. You had Black Dog, Christy Twomey and Mick O'Brien – who was a great guitar player. He'd jam with Rory when he came home and if he was playing in The Phoenix one night everyone knew he'd been jamming with Rory the night before that.

'And that was normal.'

Mick Hannigan agrees with Dorgan: 'In my late teens I remember seeing Rory Gallagher on the cover of *Melody Maker*. He'd broken the attendance record in the Marquee in London – Jimi Hendrix's old record – and that had an impact.

'We were aware of Frank O'Connor publishing in the *New Yorker*, Seán Ó Faoláin publishing in the *Playboy* – not that we ever saw a copy of *Playboy*. But Gallagher was extraordinary. Hugely successful and yet his persona, his presentation of himself was so ordinary. Plaid shirt and blue jeans, which you could go down to the Coal Quay and buy, which we did.

'There was an authenticity to him – to his music, to himself. It wasn't about glamour or tawdriness, it was rooted, which made it all the more admirable. Anywhere we could tap into the wider changes in society, we did. I remember buying a copy of *Newsweek* around the time of Woodstock and there was an article on how to tie-dye your T-shirt. Myself and my mates bought the dyes and the T-shirts, went home and carried out what seemed like a scientific experiment – in my mother's pot, bubbling away, with elastic bands around the T-shirt, and suddenly we were hippies.'

Dorgan and Hannigan would become crucial to the city's cultural life in the 1980s. The poet and the cinephile would reject the stuffy conventions to revitalise the Film Festival in particular, but Dorgan is keen to point out that they weren't sowing in a barren field.

'My mother and father met at the opera, and the next day he cancelled his ticket for Australia.

'People coming to the festival knew this was a cine-literate audience, and Cork has always had a strong theatre tradition. Most Irish writers who'd achieved anything were reliant on Dublin, which is still true to a certain extent.

'In terms of the visual arts, though, the Crawford [Art Gallery] had remarkable artists already at that stage – Alice Maher, Paul Cotter, James Scanlon – we were suddenly developing a visual culture we'd never had. The generation before them, the Charlie Tyrrells and Mick Cullens, Mick Mulcahys, they were the first revolutionary generation of the visual arts.

'You had people like Jim O'Driscoll and Gerry Goldberg and Charlie Hennessy who were great collectors and patrons. Derek Geraghty was a radio officer in the Irish Navy who'd buy paintings in the Triskel on the never-never – when he'd come home he'd hop on his motorbike to come in and look at his painting.

'People talk about the digital revolution now, but the paper-back revolution, which came before that, was just as important. In the youth culture of the time somebody, somewhere had a copy of that Andy Warhol interview, you could borrow it from them in the Long Valley and read it; everybody read the *NME*, you could talk about books and paintings and music. Irish Jack was a figure coming in and out of Cork, when he wasn't advising Pete Townsend on Who lyrics.

'I think that old Cork inferiority complex was a thing of the past. We just felt it was a grand-sized city to live in. I remember discovering that Cork then was the same size as the Athens of Pericles. So there was a critical mass. Nobody thought you were odd if you were at a session in the Phoenix one night and at the opening of an exhibition in the Triskel the following evening.

'All that seemed to dissolve overnight in a particular generation – there was still resistance in an older generation, but luminary figures like Charlie Hennessy or Gerald Goldberg stood out, and they enjoyed meeting up with the young turks.'

The reference to the Triskel is no accident. Though it was a movable feast for much of the 1970s, the arts centre was a hugely significant factor in the city's cultural landscape.

'Robbie McDonald came up with the idea of the Triskel Arts Centre out of the old Tubular Gallery, which was up those stone stairs at the side of Paul's Hairdresser's in Paul Street,' says Dorgan. 'The first one, Pat Mc [surname?] used to hand in his dole to Canada Life to pay the rent on the place in Beasley Street, but we lost that because the butter warehouse across the road went on fire and the place ended up three feet deep in butter. So that was Triskel One gone.

'Triskel Two was under what's now Pronuptia, so that was actually beneath the river level. Triskel Three was behind the Mercier Bookshop on Bridge Street, and then we found this old warehouse on Tobin Street. We got the money from the Arts Council to develop it – but then we immediately ran into "old Cork". As in, "how come ye got the money?"'

This 'old Cork' perspective was at once both simple snobbery and basic laziness. Dorgan can pinpoint the moment when he encountered what he termed the apotheosis of this attitude.

'It happened one night when I was out in Douglas. I used to go out there to visit Nancy McCarthy, who was Frank O'Connor's great love. Nancy had a pharmacy in Douglas – and was a one-woman renaissance, really – so I'd visit her for a chat.

'One evening I missed my bus home so I went into a pub for a hot whiskey – a bitter winter's night – and this … banking or insurance suit at the counter, late thirties, turned around, saw me and said, "you're one of those Triskel chappies".

'Now, when a Cork guy in a suit calls you a "chappy" he's lost the plot, but he went on: "A few of us were talking the other day – nobody knows your families, so my advice to you is to cool your jets until you know who's who and what's what in Cork."

'I must have had murder in my face, because the barman reached across the counter and put his hand on mine and said, "young fella boy" – that real Cork double-up, which I love – "he's not worth it". By the look on my face he must have thought I was going to deck your man.

'But that was the crossover moment for me in its own strange way. Robbie's father had been O/C of Collins Barracks, but that idea of "nobody knows your family" – well, good, that was our attitude.

'Apart from the Ballet Company, which was already heading for a bruising, it was the first time that an arts organisation had drawn state money into Cork, effectively. And the fact that it was a bunch of nobodies who'd done it, nobody understood that.'

What they had done was to work out how to use the system while running the Triskel, and as Dorgan puts it, they worked that out fast.

'There were five councillors on the culture subcommittee of Cork Corporation at the time, and we had them in to open the first five exhibitions we held. We also spoke to Joe McHugh, then the city manager – we explained what we were trying to do and he responded. It's not like we were gobdaws going around trying to pull the house down around us: our attitude was "the city needs this asset and it's going to have to be supported out of public funds, so who do we speak to?"

'What we did, which was unheard of, was simple – we then went and spoke to those people. We didn't get someone to talk to someone to talk to someone for us, and then six months after that you can talk to the person you should be talking to at the start … that nonsense, which only really serves to make a whole stratum of people feel important.

'Our attitude was "who's the one who makes the decision? We'll talk to them. We won't try to con them or bluff them, we'll make our case about the value of what we're trying to do and if they see that, fine."

'We were trying to sell what we wanted to do, but we weren't lying about it. We meant what we said. We said "we'll do this and do that" and again, that was unheard of at the time.'

Dorgan's view of the context is interesting, given his juxta-position of 'O'Malley's children', those who availed of Donogh O'Malley's introduction of free secondary-school education in the late 1960s, and an older, influential cohort within the city. The former influenced the latter more than might have been expected.

'This was the late 1970s, so by the early 1980s we were getting traction, and we were developing the building to some extent. It was tiny, but it's amazing what you can do if you involve people and outsource things.

'We had great credibility with visual artists, for instance, through Robbie – he was into sculpture – so we were bringing in young nationally known painters to Cork. Tony O'Malley had a big retrospective in the Crawford, and in 1985 we had Cork Art Now, a huge group show in the Crawford and the Triskel. There was a synergy building.

'That was mostly O'Malley's children, people coming through on the basis of Donogh O'Malley's decision on secondary education in the late 1960s – our contemporaries were opening galleries and spaces in Amsterdam and Ohio, and it was a rock-and-roll moment – but rock and roll with its head screwed on at the same time.

'The trick was if you weren't looking for a job, if you could get by without that but you were looking for satisfaction in your life, there were a million things that you could do and nobody could stop you. There was no competition.

'And we met older people that you might consider quite conservative who took the attitude, "we'll give it a go". The likes of Hugh Coveney and Joe McHugh, for instance, were very supportive.'

City manager McHugh taught Dorgan a valuable lesson at the time: 'When it came to change, you had to start from scratch, and Joe fought bitterly – he wanted to pedestrianise Oliver Plunkett Street and the radial streets off it, and they only gave him grudging permission to pedestrianise Winthrop Street for a year.

'Next thing, a big scandalous article in the paper, headline about "manager admits to spending £100,000 on materials".

'He'd put the best of brick and stone into it, and naively I said to him at an opening in the Triskel, "you're getting a bit of flak about the pedestrianisation, Joe." He said to me, "Young Dorgan, you strike me as someone with a certain amount of promise – I'm going to give you an idea of how things actually work. Do you think there's any one of them going to turn around and say in a year's time to put £100,000-worth of stuff in the dump out in the Carrigrohane Road?"

'Gotcha. And he got it done. They weren't going to tell him to dig it up. The lesson for us was that it was better to ask for forgiveness than permission. Everybody gets that now, but back then it was a novelty.'

The younger generation helped to raise standards in Cork, and when one of the core characters came back from England they were ready for the next stage.

'Robbie would kill me for saying this,' says Dorgan, 'But when Ger Donovan left the Crawford Art Gallery and there was an advertisement to replace him, he went for it, and the response was, "why are you going for that when you've only just gotten the Triskel off the ground?"

'His answer was, "I know, but once it's known that I've applied for this you'll at least have to hire someone better qualified than me to run the Crawford." 'And he was dead right. They got Peter Murray in, who did a great job for years.

'There was a perception we were brash, but we didn't care about that. We weren't into taking no for an answer, and we didn't feel we had to be beholden to anyone.

'We learned, too, as we went along. I learned about paintings from hanging canvases with Robbie for exhibitions. We ran poetry readings. And then Mick Hannigan came back from England and became the film programmer.'

Hannigan took Dorgan's views on doing a million things you wanted to do if you didn't want a job and put them into practice.

'I got involved with the Triskel in 1985 under the social employment scheme, which was a far-thinking move then. I read about it in the *Examiner* and went to the FÁS office and spoke to a progressive guy there, pointing the scheme out to him.

'You got double the dole for twenty hours a week working on the scheme, which meant the state was acknowledging there was social merit in people working on socially valuable projects – building walls, clearing parks, or artistic events.

'He hadn't been fully briefed on it but he took out a ledger, took my name and address for the scheme and put me in the ledger for it – the first person in Cork to apply.

I then went to the Triskel, where I used to hang around anyway, and said "if you guys want to do films I can do that for you and it won't cost you a penny." Robbie McDonald said to send in a proposal, I wrote a couple of pages, Theo looked over it and tarted it up, and then Robbie said, "that's grand". I was employed to run a film club.'

Politically aware, Hannigan points out that the early 1980s was a high point, of sorts, in terms of American foreign policy, as evidenced by the Sandinista scarves then beloved of many students. Film in Cork was an unlikely beneficiary of the US Department of State.

'This was a time of great turmoil in terms of American foreign policy – Nicaragua and all of that, American imperialism was a term that tripped off the tongue.

'A new cultural attaché was appointed to the American Embassy in Dublin whose previous posting had been in South America – a very interesting man, and given the links between the US secret services and the arts, traditionally, funding all sorts of avant garde movements, *Encounter* magazine and so on, it was all the more interesting.

'For instance, the first Kenneth Anger films I saw were screened at the Crawford by this cultural attaché chap – on 16mm – with a very insightful introduction to these experimental films.

'Around this time there was a change in film-projection technology – you didn't have the traditional projector as such, it was essentially an LP version of the film, like an old record album. A friend of mine thought this was the future, as it happens, and invested a lot of his own money in buying these up.

'You got an hour of film from each side, for the second half of the film you had to turn it over – just like an LP – and our friend from the embassy contacted the Film Festival saying he had thirty American classics in that version – *Citizen Kane* and the like – if they were interested. The festival was interested – they were free – but the catch was that because of rights issues, you couldn't charge admission to see the films. It had to be free.'

The Film Festival contacted Triskel, who had Hannigan on board, having set up a film club.

'That entailed having someone on the door and making sure the venue was clear and – the main job – was to turn over the album-film and put the stylus down properly on the other side.

'We had packed houses, of course, because these were free to festival members, and you could get membership for a couple of quid. So at a time when festival attendances were going down, here was the Triskel packing them in.

'Of course we were, the films were free, but the perception was abroad that the fuddy-duddies in the festival had lost touch and the young whippersnappers at the Triskel had the magic touch.

'That was totally unfair – I was employed to do that job and they weren't, and as I say, there was no charge for the films we were showing. The Triskel was a new venue as well, so you had all of those factors coming into play.'

The Cork Film Festival dates back to 1956 and was the brainchild of Dermot Breen; it was one of the first film festivals recognised by the International Federation of Film Producers' Associations and as such it had a considerable reputation in its early decades.

Total attendance at the festival in those days could top the 30,000 mark, and at various periods, the likes of director Otto Preminger and actors James Mason and Boris Karloff came to Cork.

It's telling, however, that the festival story which proved most durable was that of Dawn Addams, a starlet who famously demanded a bathtub of milk in 1957. That Addams is remembered solely for her dairy requests tells its own story, as perhaps does the fact that festival director Breen would go on to start Cork's first PR agency.

By the 1980s the festival was tired and in decline: 'sclerotic' was the term used by Hannigan, and it is difficult to disagree with that description. Film buff that he was, he didn't go to the festival.

'I'm not blaming the festival for this, but I felt it wasn't for me. That it was an event for the bourgeoisie of Cork.

'I remember my father taking me down outside the old Savoy Cinema to watch the stars arrive for the festival in their limousines. Looking back now, were they stars? Often they were Rank starlets, brought over to do outrageous things for photographs, the Dawn Addams-type stunts.

'For whatever reason – mainly my own skewed perception – I felt it wasn't for me, anyway. My film appreciation came from the UCC Film Society, which was a huge resource – every Wednesday night and Sunday night of term, you'd see the best movies.

'Then I moved to London and would go to the Electric on the Portobello Road, the Academy Cinema in Oxford Street – I had world cinema available to me through any number of other routes, and I felt I was up to speed with what was happening in European cinema. The 1970s was an amazing period in Hollywood as well, Bob Rafelson, Scorsese, all of those new directors.

'But I never saw the festival as a way into that. In my teens and early twenties I'd have felt Cork generally was parochial and self-satisied. Smug, really.

'That whole insular "who do they think they are to tell us what to do", that attitude pushed me and my mates to look elsewhere – to look outside for influences in terms of Paris '68, the anti-war movement in the States, and to make connections between our small corner of the world and the larger movements outside it.'

How could they make that connection with the Film Festival, however?

21

Ford Save the Projector

I t was the 1984 Cork Film Festival when everything came to a head.

'We were sitting up in the balcony for one of the films,' says Theo Dorgan. 'Myself, Mick Hannigan and Robbie McDonald, when it was announced that the festival was in trouble.

'We looked at each other and said, "we're not going to let that happen, are we?

'When you think of it, the cheek of us – "we're not going to let that happen", when we hadn't a red cent to our name – but we moved fast. Mick and myself sat down in what's now Larry Tompkins' bar and decided we'd take it on. Over three pints of Murphy's we decided.'

The training with Triskel stood to them: they knew about central funding and local funding, and they had phone numbers to hand. They also had the ideal man to front the operation.

'The week of the festival the artistic director, Ronnie Saunders, resigned,' remembers Mick Hannigan. 'The game was up, really. Robin O'Sullivan had set up a PR company and was doing this voluntarily because nobody else would do it. He'd done his stint, so he resigned too.

'I remember on the Friday of the festival, in the Capitol, Charlie Hennessy gave that *cri de coeur* from the stage – he could be wonderfully theatrical when the occasion demanded it – and from my seat in the balcony I remember thinking, "what's Charlie on about?", but clearly he wanted the festival to survive.'

A couple of days after the three pints of Murphy's, Hannigan was out and about again.

'In the Festival Club up in the Imperial – very sparsely attended – I was approached by Tiernan MacBride, Seán MacBride's son, who was on the Irish Film Board and had had short films at Cannes and so on.

'He bustled over and said, "you're the next director of the festival", and I said, "Tiernan, that's very flattering, but let's be honest – I've never screened a film in my life, and …" and he barked back, "Never put yourself down."

'He introduced me to everyone that night as the next director, but when things calmed down, after the festival, Charlie came up to the Triskel to say he wanted them involved with the festival.

'And Triskel said they'd get involved and could provide an office. Now, Triskel had me, but I didn't have the self-confidence, or the experience to say I'd do this or do that. I'm not putting myself down: I didn't have that experience, but myself and Theo had organisational abilities, I knew film and he knew the media … there was a bit of kerfuffling but after an interview process Theo and I got the gig.

'The difference was we suddenly had a year-round office, and we were paid intermittently. I was getting the social employment money every week, Theo was being paid by Triskel for PR and their literature programme, and every now and again we'd be paid by the festival.'

'We talked to the Film Board and they agreed to put in ten grand,' says Dorgan. 'We talked to RTÉ and they agreed to put in ten grand, and we put it to the festival committee – we said we'd take it on and run it from the building next door to the Triskel, so all the resources of the Triskel would be available, but we'd focus on film.

'We had nothing to lose. They gave us the okay so we went back to Dick Hill, the manager in the Opera House, and negotiated terms with him.

'Mick knew film inside out, and by that time I'd learned a lot about the city and funding sources, so we were a good team. One of our first announcements was that anybody turning up with a dicky bow would be turned away.'

Hannigan gives a rational assessment of the festival as it was.

'It's important to remember that the festival was not the culture flagship of the city, then. It was in decline – certainly financially it was all over the shop. The accounts from previous years were mind-boggling, really, while attendances weren't good, programming wasn't great, the number of guests had reduced. It was on its uppers, that was the reality.

'*The Irish Times*' film critic then, Ray Comiskey, came to Cork every year for the Jazz Festival, which was his main interest, and then he became the film critic – and a very good one. And he called Cork out, in the modern phrase, a couple of times – that the festival wasn't fit for purpose, basically.

'The Irish film community had little regard for the festival as well; one member of that community once said to me that it was as though there were a wire across the county bounds and when a Dublin-based film-maker crossed it, an alarm went off. There was a feeling they weren't welcome.

'Maybe the Cork bourgeoisie, who ran the festival and were protective about it, had an attitude of "who are you to come down and tell us what to do, we're an international festival, don't you know?", that kind of thing.

'They were trading on past successes, though. Looking back at references to past glamour at the festival, when you looked at it, it was a tawdry glamour. Francois Truffaut came with Jean-Pierre Léaud and *The 400 Blows*, Vittorio Visconti came, there were some great international figures – but subsequently it seemed to be British TV stars. Very much second division.

'That's not a criticism, because the Cork Film Festival would be in the second division of the film festival ecology. There are A-standard festivals and B-standard festivals. Years ago you had to go to an organisation called FIAPF to get accreditation as a film festival, which is what Cork did; it was one of the first such festivals in the world, but it was still a B-list festival, and that's being descriptive, not disparaging. But even allowing for that, it had slipped back a good deal. The people running it were enthusiastic amateurs, as they described themselves – there was no full-time office or secretariat, for instance.'

At one stage the Arts Council pulled the plug financially and took whatever assets there were left: the film projector, in this case. In parallel with that, however, the Irish Film Board (IFB) was established and Muiris Mac Conghail, who chaired it, took the view that the Cork Film Festival could not be allowed to die – so when the Arts Council pulled funding, the IFB stepped in and provided funding.

'The Council still owned the projector, though,' says Hannigan. 'For a lot of good reasons the festival moved from the Opera

House to the Capitol – the projector had originally been bought for the Opera House, back in the 1970s. It had only been used for a few years. You might think it a waste of money, but the alternative was to hire one every year. They clearly thought of it as an asset at the time, and they bought a screen and a speaker as well, a considerable investment. The Opera House was precluded from screening films by some statute anyway.'

'The festival was already dead at that stage,' Dorgan recalls. 'It was like a tree that's dead at the roots but the head's still above ground.

'It had been a brilliant idea when Der Breen set it up in the fifties – at that stage it was only the fifth licensed film festival in the world. They were ahead of the posse, and in those days glamour was the antidote to poverty.

'But it had become sclerotic. People were driving into town to the festival club and not even bothering to go to the films themselves. The programming had become *leadránach*, to say the least.

'We made some interesting discoveries when we took over. We got a message from SovExport Films which read: 'Greetings Cork Film Festival, the films we will send you this year are …' And we sent back a telex – a telex! – from RTÉ Union Quay saying: "No, under new management, in due course we will inform you of what films we wish to request." And there was murder! We had to go to London to meet them to sort it out. It was stressful but we had to do it. We wanted to show the most interesting films, to reach out to the Irish film community and to show short films.

'One of Mick's great successes in the years that followed was to build the festival so deeply into the community of Irish film-makers and distributors, producers, directors and actors, that they came to think of it as their own.'

Hannigan echoes the story of the film company seeking to impose its own selections on the festival: 'That's not how you run a film festival: it should be the other way around.

'The festival was in decline, certainly, but there were good things there. The year before we took over, there was a Richard Attenborough retrospective and he came over and did a public interview, which was commendable. And then there was Kenneth Griffith, who made a film about Michael Collins called *Hang Up Your Brightest Colours* and another, *Curious Journey*, which was an oral history of the old IRA in west Cork. Important work.

'*Curious Journey* was later published in book form – a great read, first-hand testimony. The films were screened in the Lee Cinema at half nine or ten on a Tuesday morning, and I always regret missing them, because the cinema was packed with those old IRA guys.

'Griffith owned those films because UTV refused to broadcast them on account of their content. After they stalled and stalled, Griffith bought the films back from them – but I'm giving those examples because it shows there were good things going on, even though the festival was in decline.

'Everybody loves a fresh start, so that was the narrative: new blood, fresh energy, new posters, young guys getting involved – although we were in our thirties at that stage, even – back to the Opera House … all the naive bluster that comes with a new start.'

They set down a marker early on. The year before they took over, Dorgan recalls, John T. Davis had had *Shellshock Rock* refused: 'Our response was to have a John T. Davis season – all of his films. So we were giving a certain message.

'The opening night of our first festival, in 1985, we filled the Opera House and turned away 200 people. And they'd had 230 at the closing night the year before.

'It wasn't because we were geniuses, though Mick was very, very good on cinema, but this was a cultured city. People knew culture and they wanted to feel welcome at the festival, which was the key thing. The *Examiner* described the crowd as punks to pensioners, and it was right.

'I remember there was nobody there from *The Irish Times* so I photocopied an Ordnance Survey map and wrote on it, at Naas, "there is life south of this line" and faxed it to their office, to the arts editor. And in fairness, a fax came back with "point taken, reporter en route".

'Our attitude was "nobody's unwelcome, but we're taking no prisoners." We showed tough films and challenged the audience. That was a feature of the festival under Mick's direction, but why not when there was an audience willing to go with you? There was plenty of fun involved – the Festival Club was a good laugh.'

And the dicky bow rule?

'We didn't really turn away anyone in a dicky bow. Nobody came along wearing one, but if they had we'd have invited them in, certainly.

'I think Triskel opened the ground and the Film Festival grew out of that. But we'd learned our arts management skills on the job with those; there were no degree courses in that area to be found. The people in black polo necks and designer specs hadn't materialised quite yet.

'We learned by doing. If it's five minutes to opening and there's dirt on the floor, you get a brush and sweep it up – you don't ask "who's in charge of this?"

'There was also that first naive flush of enthusiasm. A huge amount of it was down to Robbie McDonald, whose attitude was always "cheerful service", with an equal emphasis on both words. His view was always "why not? We'll try this". It broke down the school-born idea that the arts were a reserved mystery.

'Take any street in Cork. There isn't a house where there aren't a couple of lads in a band, or someone learning the fiddle, or someone who's passionate about going to the movies, or acting … it's a natural part of life. We started from the proposition that when people aren't wage slaves or looking for the ride, what they mostly turn to are sports and the arts.'

The year 1985 was a low point in a decade of low points in the city. Dorgan and Hannigan were very conscious of the closures, one of which had a direct impact on the festival.

'For ease of reference people divide a city into groups or areas or classes, but we all lived in the same place. We were well aware of what was happening.

'Ford's had given a few bob towards the film festival, and when they were closing down, Charlie Hennessy arranged for Mick and me to go down to the factory to meet Hartmut Kieven. He was the guy sent in to close the factory, and he did so brutally but efficiently. The Ford way.

'We went down to look for sponsorship. There was a lot of chat, there were photographs taken by Billy Mills of him signing the cheque … I looked down at the cheque and looked at Mick. At ten past one we were outside the AIB at 66 South Mall and at half past we had the cheque lodged.'

The amount on the cheque was a good deal more than they had anticipated. Mick Hannigan has a slightly different take on the meeting in the Marina, but the disparity in funding remains pretty constant.

'When Ford's closed, Charlie had some meeting with the company CEO – he wasn't Irish, or American, I think he was from the European end of the operation, maybe Germany or France. Kieven Hart, Charlie, Theo and I went down to Ford's as it was closing because Charlie had secured sponsorship from them, and in the office, as this chap was literally poised with his pen over the chequebook, he said, 'How much was it again?''

"'£25,000,' said Charlie.

'Your man signed it and we left with the cheque.

'To this day I don't know where Charlie got that figure. I think he just blurted it out. There was a process, presumably, which involved negotiations and phone calls before that day, but whether or which, we left the factory that day with a cheque for twenty-five grand.

'That paid for the rental of the Opera House, which was a significant cost, and for marketing and so on.'

And the film projector?

'And the film projector.'

It wasn't long before the man who signed the cheque realised his error.

'Next thing, a panicky phone call,' says Dorgan.

'He was saying he thought it was £1,000, not £10,000, and so on, and I said, "we're very grateful for the cheque but you know and I know that this is conscience money: you put 1,000 people in the city out of work and you got a wraparound in the local paper thanking you. Let's not lose the run of ourselves. Tell me, how would you like to deal with a headline in the *Examiner* tomorrow, 'Ford asks for its money back'?"

'There was a pause and he said, "you're a tough guy", and he hung up.'

Dorgan points out that Ford still got their money's worth for the sponsorship.

'We put their logo on the poster – not too big, though in fairness we gave the poster designers, who would work on stuff for the Marquee in London later, all of them, we gave them their head and some of it was probably gawky, but it worked out.

'At the time, we'd pick up people for the festival at the airport and Kieven came through one night, flanked by some of the under-managers from Ford, the Montenotte mafia, and he saw

193

the poster for the festival, and he saw me waiting for someone or other: "Ach, we should have argued for a bigger presence for our logo on the poster."

"'Now, now," I said, "we've had the conversation about conscience money already."

'His colleagues pitched in with "excuse me, come here now", but Kieven cut them off: "No, no, this is the first honest Corkman I have met."'

Dorgan points out that the car manufacturer's connection to the festival was not always a confrontation.

'In fairness to Ford, they gave us five Grenadas to swan the guests for the festival around in, and we'd have these lads from Collins Barracks taking a week's leave to do the driving, great characters.

'And this was important, too. Those guys were important because they'd been doing that for years. They'd driven everybody over the years who'd come to Cork for the festival, and they knew just how to deal with them – if they had a spare half-hour and the visitor was interested, they'd bring them around the city on a tour, and you could leave them off to it. They were part of the memory of the festival and they were your prime ambassadors because they were spending so much time with these actors and directors and whatever.

'One guy, Donie, from Mulgrave Road, was brilliant. We had great volunteers, the likes of Vita Green, who'd been coming in for years, but we also had eighteen- and nineteen-year-olds, and it worked well – the young kids were mad about the older crowd, and the older crowd thought the young kids were great.'

Soon the whole crowd of them would be famous, thanks to one of the most controversial films of the decade.

22

Down With This Sort of Thing

Mick Hannigan's general view of the Film Festival as a night out for the Cork middle classes needs some amendment, by his own admission. He had some history of his own with the Festival, after all. A history which involved a brief spell behind bars.

'I'd been to the Festival once before, to see *The China Syndrome*. I was working in England and came back to discover there were plans for a nuclear power plant to be built in Carnsore Point.

'I got involved in a small group which opposed the plant, and we had weekly meetings about it. Some of them were tedious because I had no great interest in science and the meeting might be all about nuclear fission or whatever, the economics of the plant.

'At one meeting I pointed out the festival was going to screen *The China Syndrome*, which of course dealt with an accident at a nuclear power plant in the States, an earnest ecological thriller. At the time it was released there was a real-life nuclear accident at a power plant, in Three Mile Island, life imitating art, and I said to the group, "this is a great opportunity for us" but there wasn't too much interest.

'I knew enough about politics and propaganda to work a Gestetner machine, so I wrote up an earnest warning to the people of Ireland, drawing their attention to similarities between Three Mile Island and Carnsore Point – the thing wrote itself – and then ran off flyers with the text.'

The rest of Hannigan's group were busy on the evening the film was shown, so he headed off on his own to the showing, half an hour early, to give out the flyers.

'A young woman came up to me who turned out to be an American Quaker, and she helped me to give them out. I didn't know her from Adam, but she was helping me when the rest of the group weren't even there.

'I was handing them out in the foyer of the Opera House when the manager came up to me and said, "Sorry now, I have to ask you to leave, this is private property." He was a gentleman. Dick Hill. Very charming. Out I went onto the footpath in front, which I thought was a public thoroughfare.

'Anyway, a guy from the festival came out – tuxedo, the whole deal – and told me to "go away now". I said I was doing nothing wrong – I wasn't complaining to people or getting in their way, just pointing out parallels between Three Mile Island and Carnsore Point.

'Some people were taking the leaflets, some weren't, as they passed me in their evening gowns and tuxedos, but then I was grabbed by a garda.'

By his own admission Hannigan reacted badly.

'I resisted arrest. He wanted me to get into the squad car, I wouldn't, I was shouting "I'm being arrested for nothing" and so on, and I threw the flyers up in the air.

'I should have just accepted I was arrested and that the garda was doing his duty as he saw it, but I didn't. I saw it as a huge infringement of my civil liberties and my right to free speech, and I wouldn't co-operate, and the garda didn't know what to do.

'He couldn't get me into the squad car, and I couldn't be given a whack because it was outside the Opera House and there were probably photographers there, so they walked me up the quay to the Bridewell. The manager came after us saying "we don't want him arrested" but the garda said "well, it's too late for that now."

'Anyway, I ran out of steam up in the Bridewell. They took some details, I was put in a cell.'

Unfortunately, the cell could not be locked by the garda, so Hannigan had to help with his own incarceration.

'I pulled it shut after me and locked it. It wasn't too pleasant in the cell but I was let out after twenty minutes or half an hour, with a "you'll be hearing from us" from the Gardaí.

'I went back up the quay and was in time for the film, so I went in, and afterwards I was surrounded by people, including a couple of journalists, so it was represented in the *Examiner*. The caption for the photo accompanying the piece was "Bearded Anti-Nuclear Protestor ..." I called out to Theo the following Monday and he was saying, "ah, my bearded and protesting friend ..."

'There was a court case and I was accused of resisting arrest, which was true, and maybe assaulting a garda, which wasn't, though I could see why they'd have said that, and behaviour likely to lead to a breach of the peace. Those are the charges I remember.

I was found guilty in the district court and my solicitor appealed, and Blaise O'Carroll, the barrister, got me off on a point of law, so the case was struck out.

'I raise that because it shows that the festival was showing films which passed comment on the issues of the time, but there was that fissure between those in tuxedos who were attending and those who had other politics.

'I've no doubt that the chap who objected to what I was doing was acting according to his own lights to protect the festival, but any festival like that should welcome the opportunity to resonate deep within people's lives, not just operate in a rarefied way.

'That was emblematic of the fissure. It just so happened that I was the person in the middle at that time. And the odd time in later years, when I got involved with the festival, someone would say to me, "aren't you the guy ...?" and I'd say, "yeah, I am."'

If you have seen *Father Ted* you remember, no doubt, the episode when a controversial film is shown at the local cinema – *The Passion of St Tibulus* – and Fr Ted and Co. are deputed to protest at the screening. The priests' placards certainly lived long in the memory ('Down with this sort of thing') but the incident carried an echo of one of Mick Hannigan's more notorious selections for the Cork Film Festival.

There was an accepted code for art films that might have been a little racy for the Ireland of the mid 1980s. Terms such as 'frank', 'earthy', 'unexpurgated' – even 'French' – would suggest the possibility of exposed flesh and attendances could spike sharply for the most unlikely films which carried those descriptions in a catalogue.

The Last Temptation of Christ, directed by Martin Scorsese, was no art-house obscurity, however, when it was confirmed for the Cork Film Festival of 1988. It was widely known that the film starred Willem Dafoe as Jesus who, in his final hours, would contemplate an alternative life in which he had married Mary Magdalene, played by Barbara Hershey. More to the point, there were scenes in which the marriage was consummated.

When the film played in Godless Paris, a cinema was set on fire and closed for three years because of the damage, while in Cork, three years earlier, moving statues had been seen in Ballinspittle. How would Cork react to seeing Jesus have sex on the thirty-foot screen of the Opera House?

'*The Last Temptation* was certainly memorable,' says Mick Hannigan. 'There were objections to the film all over the world, but there was a previous incident when Ronnie Saunders, the preceding director, had gone to Cannes to see a Godard film, *Je Vous Salue Marie*, which created a lot of controversy with a naked Christ and some sex scenes.

'Some journalist had asked Ronnie if this would figure at the Cork Film Festival and he said something to the effect that he hoped so, and there was a huge controversy about it, letters coming in to the festival in green ink – "God bless ye, ye heathens".

'That was a given every year – the *Examiner* journalists would scour the programme for "the controversial one" they could get a headline out of. I wouldn't play that game, but when *The Last Temptation* came up ... There were board meetings about it, there was opposition, but we won the day.'

An *Examiner* journalist rang Hannigan about the film and he got the truth.

'He asked and I said we were going to show it, but asked him to hold it for a few days; he said he would, and did, but he was scooped by a radio station. He probably should have told me he couldn't sit on it. I always regretted that, because he was decent enough to hold it.

199

'Charlie, Theo and I went to London to see the film – in a packed house, as you can imagine – but the distributor asked us would we screen it on the basis, I'd say, that he'd see what the lie of the land was after we took the heat in Cork with the first screening.'

The screening duly turned into an event. Buses came from Ballinspittle and Ballyvourney with people who paraded in front of the Opera House saying the rosary, and there was a counter-demonstration by students, some of them dressed in cod-biblical clothing. Television news crews filmed the two groups, and the visibly embarrassed festival goers queuing beyond them.

'The opposition outside the Opera House on the night, it was from that sector of Catholicism … people who use religion as therapy, or support,' says Hannigan. 'They're simple, ordinary people who have faith and who rely on that faith. My point is that the right-wing Catholics, the letter writers, if you like, stayed well away.

'I was asked to come in to RTÉ to defend the decision to show the film, and next to me was the diocesan press officer. I took a measured approach – "Scorsese is a major director, this is not pornography but a serious film, it doesn't intend to offend, etc.," and the press officer was batting for his side, although he admitted he hadn't seen it, so he was on a bit of a sticky wicket.

The Bishop of Cork at the time was Michael Murphy, and all he did was to advise his flock not to go to the film, which seemed a very reasonable line to take. As I said on air, adding that I had no argument with the bishop whatsoever.

'It was all very reasonable as an exchange of views, no rancour or snideness.'

The interview had an odd sequel, though. After they finished in the studio the diocesan press officer asked Hannigan he could see the film.

'I said we didn't have a tape to hand but I offered him tickets; he said he couldn't be seen to go in but I offered to slip him in the back door of the Opera House the night of the screening.

'I arranged to meet him at the back of the Opera House and let him in for the showing. And at half eleven I met him at the stage door, very cloak and dagger – he knocked and I let him in. He was hidden in one of the boxes upstairs, and he might still be there for all I know. I never saw him again, but he saw it from up there.'

Hannigan didn't have much sympathy with the students who pitched up outside the Opera House.

'A group of Crawford Art College students came down to counter-demonstrate, which was a bit of a spoof. Satire should always punch upwards, but on the night they were punching downwards. The people protesting were sincere Catholics, and they were having a vigil: they weren't objecting. They were an easy target for the students, who dressed up in mock-Palestinian clothing, one of them was dressed as the Virgin Mary.

'One of their placards read "Jesus was nailed, not screwed", and there was a shot of one of the religious people trying to tear that down. It was a bit unfair – here you had students having a laugh at sincere people – but the image was very good, because within that image you have conflict.'

As for the movie itself …

'It was a flop. RTÉ were there on the night – we showed it at midnight and they had cameras there when the audience started coming out at around three a.m. Tom McSweeney was their reporter and he spotted an old lady coming down the stairs from the showing and he went straight over: "What did you think of the film?"

"'It was okay," she said, "Quite slow and drawn-out. I don't know what all the fuss was about." That's what went out on the six o'clock news the following evening, and the nine o'clock news. What Tom didn't realise at the time that that was my mother, who was then in her seventies.'

Mrs Hannigan's review of the film was accurate (it *is* slow and drawn out) but her common-sense answer rather defused the sense of Ireland on the cusp of a new era of debauchery. Her own focus was far closer to home.

'She was a daily Mass goer and her main concern the day after those news broadcasts was the reaction she'd receive at ten a.m. Mass the following day in Blackpool, that she might be shunned.

'She went down and sat in her usual place, and afterwards all she heard was "you looked lovely on the telly last night". The content didn't matter, the appearance was all that counted.

'That was a highlight.'

23

The Field on the Boreenmanna Road

Cork made the All-Ireland senior hurling final in 1984 with an experienced team. Unfortunately, much of that recent experience had been negative: the team had lost the previous two All-Ireland finals to Kilkenny and were trying to avoid the unwanted distinction of becoming the first team to lose three All-Ireland finals in a row.

They were not sheltered from what had been happening in Cork. On the contrary, the closures and catastrophes were mentioned in the dressing room with a view to inspiring the players. The city needed a lift, they were told; they could provide it with a win.

They won comfortably, 3-16 to 1-12.

'One Sunday, the two crossed,' says Theo Dorgan of the great Leeside interests. 'Any country that had a film in the festival, the tradition was that you hung that country's flag outside the

Opera House, so you had all these national flags flying near the bridge. Among our films one year was one which had been shot clandestinely in South Africa, so we flew the ANC flag – black, green and yellow – rather than the official flag.

'Myself and Mick were standing outside when this chap strolled up to us: 'Fair dues to ye, fair dues, it would take two Blackpool boys to have the Glen flag flying from the Opera House on a day like this.'

'The Glen had won the county final. I hadn't the heart to point out that I was Na Piarsaigh all my life, but I suppose it was an ecumenical matter.'

A stubborn narrative sprang up after a decisive event in 1980s Cork sport. The sale of Flower Lodge on the Boreenmanna Road to the GAA was refashioned as a betrayal in the way the departure of Ford was a betrayal: the great soccer playing surface stolen away by the devious Gaels of the GAA, a theft aided and abetted by the FAI's neglectful attitude.

Plunkett Carter, doyen of Cork sports historians, is the ideal man to offer a wider perspective on the time. That perspective has to take in the 1970s first, though.

'You're never going to have a 1972 again, when everything came together. The following season Cork Hibs, after winning a great FAI Cup, packing Flower Lodge out, were on for another promising season and got to the Cup final – but only got 12,000 people at it. In Cork.

'That was the sign. There was an apathy there, beginning around that time. It started in Dublin, where there were serious difficulties, but that year, 1973, ruined it for Cork because we were always saying, "give us the big games", and when we did …

'We weren't going to get them – even when we had an international in the 1980s, again the attendance was disappointing, 12,000 people or so.

'Cork people gave you a chance. They'd watch the games at the start of the season, and if you had a strong team and people thought you had a chance, they'd come out. Now, they'd skip the Shield competition and come back for the League.

'But they knew in the 1970s, they could see from the quality of the players coming in that the team would be there or thereabouts – but there or thereabouts wasn't good enough. The team had to be winning, to be seen as going to win it or challenge.

'And it just fell off. What really showed that was when Cork Celtic fell back on the old ploy, bringing in a big name. They brought in George Best.'

Best lined out for Cork against Drogheda in 1975 and the take at the gate was £6,000. It was a time-honoured way of raising funds, but one that was fatally flawed.

'They made a killing out of that – there's no doubt they made money out of it – but the week before Best came in they'd had a great win up in Drogheda and then they nosedived.

'Players were in awe of Best and didn't know about playing their own positions, because they knew the crowd was there to see Best, for instance, so they felt they had to bring him into the game.

'After three games he was gone, but financially it assured the club for the rest of the year.'

Decades before Best's arrival it had been a fail-safe mechanism to keep a League of Ireland team on the road.

'See, there was always a slur on football in Cork going back … well, you couldn't go back to Fordson's, that was just a decision made then that they didn't want to be associated with professional football any longer.

'After that they became Cork United, and a United Nations team, pulling in players from all over Britain with the promise of jobs in Ford's, for instance.

'Cork United won five leagues and two Cups in seven years, and they pulled in an attendance for one game of over 30,000 for a league game … and yet they claimed they weren't making money, that they were losing money every season.

'They were pulling maybe 3,000, maybe 7,000 for bigger games, but the regular attendances weren't the vast crowds we were told about. What happened was they were paying top dollar when they went away for games and overnighted. For Cup finals they'd spend a week in Bray getting ready for the game.

'Some of United's former players – Donie Madden, Florrie Burke – became directors with Cork Athletic and carried that on. They paid Raich Carter £50 a week at a time when footballers in England were getting £11 a week, and of course they won the league.

'But after that they fell off as well. Boom and bust again, it couldn't be sustained.'

That lesson was forgotten, however, in the afterglow of the Best gates.

'That was always the plan when you were in trouble – to get a big name in to boost the crowds – but the experience with Best messed that up. When Geoff Hurst came in after that the attendances were 3,000, whereas there'd been crowds of 9,000 for Best.

'Ian Callaghan, Trevor Brooking, Terry McDermott – they were all one-game wonders. Uwe Seeler was another one who played for Celtic. Michael O'Connell was the big Adidas man in Cork and he got friendly with Seeler in Germany, where he was working with Adidas, and Seeler got the impression that he was coming over to play in an exhibition to raise funds for the club, not a league game. In fairness to him, he was very good. Four years earlier he was top scorer in the Bundesliga, and he got two of the greatest goals ever seen in Turner's Cross. It would have been three, a fantastic hat trick, only Bertie O'Sullivan ran across his boot while waiting to hit a volley, and he hit Bertie instead.

'I think Seeler regretted playing the game afterwards, though, because he'd been a one-club man all his career with Hamburg, so playing for Celtic spoiled his record a little.'

They didn't last, however. Celtic folded, to be replaced by Cork Alberts; Carter points out they were essentially a junior-grade team playing in Flower Lodge, and the attendance was in the hundreds.

'The crowds vanished completely, way below average. There were attendances of less than 2,000 for league games – the kind of crowd you'd have twenty years earlier for a game against a junior selection.

'People weren't fools. They could see the players were past their prime. This was Cork: people knew players weren't training, for instance. Because of that, the FAI didn't have confidence in Cork, and it was hard to blame them. Teams changed, the owners changed, so the FAI felt the people running football couldn't be trusted.'

This was significant, coming into the 1980s, particularly as the recession began to bite. The FAI's distrust often had a solid basis. In Cork United's short-lived run as the League of Ireland's representatives on Leeside, for instance, the time-honoured fail-safe method backfired badly.

'They brought over Manchester City in 1982,' says Carter. 'And City were huge at a time, but that was a misjudgement, they got it wrong in thinking they'd be an attractive proposition. They were very big at the time, but it was a Saturday afternoon in December, bad weather all that week … everything went wrong.

'And in fairness to them, they were at full strength, but Cork United were very poor. Were people going to go and watch them?

'Compare that to the basketball, which was very big then. It was glamorous, the big players could be seen around town – but also, the stadium was in the heart of the north side, and basketball was a north-side game, really.'

The downturn had an impact on soccer in the city, but not in the expected way. In some sectors there was expansion, not contraction.

'The closures didn't help, certainly. But in my view it affected places like golf clubs more, places which had big subs to pay, as opposed to £1.50 for a game every couple of weeks.

'There was a huge expansion in schoolboy soccer then because there were plenty of people available to run teams. There was one grade starting off, in the 1960s, and by 1980 there were 3,500 schoolboys, the equivalent of a 150 clubs compared to the starting base of six or seven clubs.

'You could tell by the spread of trophies. From the 1980s on, you didn't have St Mary's, Rockmount, Tramore, all of them dominating all the time. The likes of Midleton and Bandon started to come to the fore.'

Other elements helped to expand the game, he adds. *Match of the Day*, *The Big Match*, for instance, they were a big factor, and at that stage they were often on early in the evening. That sounds strange, but it meant kids could watch, and it encouraged them. In recent years people would complain that the Eircom League highlights were on at eleven p.m. on RTÉ – when would a kid see those? And Jack Charlton's success with the team later in the 1980s was another huge boost to the game.'

At the top level, however, there was nothing. After Cork United went out of existence there was no League of Ireland team in the city between 1982 and 1983. Cobh Ramblers' extraordinary run to the 1983 FAI Cup semi-final helped to fill the gap temporarily, reinforcing Carter's basic theory of Cork soccer attendances: give us crowds and we'll follow crowds.

'Cobh got a great result, and there was no soccer in Cork at the time, the next round couldn't be played in Cobh ... an attendance of around 12,000 was expected but they got twice that, and there was another replay.

'They made more money in that one match than all the teams in Cork had made in the two years before they went out of football.

'Give us crowds and we'll follow crowds – that was the way it went. You saw it at other levels: Avondale played St Mary's in the AOH [Ancient Order of Hibernians] Cup final in 1977 and there were 5,000 people at it: the highest attendance at a league game in soccer in Ireland that year. A Coventry City scout was down and I met him at the game, he couldn't get over the crowd and the slagging and so on.'

When Cork City re-formed and took the field, they did so in Flower Lodge.

'I couldn't understand that,' says Carter. 'It was a mistake. They were going to be touting for crowds and were going to struggle to create an atmosphere there, which they needed. A few hundred people, a thousand people, wouldn't be as bad in Turner's Cross, and when football came back the attendances were very low, and a lot of the players were familiar, the old faces, plus some from the Munster Senior League.

'And eventually they saw the light. They had to get out of Flower Lodge. They were saying at the time the rent was high, but I'd say a hundred people at the turnstiles would have covered the rent.

'When City went to Turner's Cross and saw the atmosphere, that 2,000 people looked great there compared to how 2,000 would look in Flower Lodge – awful, in other words – then you could see it worked.'

City's move to Turner's Cross focused minds on the recently vacated venue in Ballinlough and, in particular, why people would not go to Flower Lodge.

Carter can point to the variety of bad experiences at the venue, such as the time officials went to Flower Lodge to open the stadium for a Munster Senior Cup game that was to open the season, only to find the grass was a foot long. Literally.

'Who could cut it? They all went off in their cars and came back with their home lawn mowers, and they managed to cut the pitch.

'The game went on even though the markings were all off line and uneven, there were heaps of grass everywhere, it was cut short here and was still long over here … the fact that it was a Munster Senior Cup tie with local teams meant officials turned a blind eye to it, but that was very poor. There was always something.

'The AOH themselves played there, and they had a junior team; the players loved playing there but that was the extent of their connection with the Lodge. Tramore Athletic used it, too, but at the end of the day it was a ghost stadium. The numbers going to some of the matches would have fitted into the dugouts with the substitutes, really.

'What made Flower Lodge so unattractive? I don't know. Turner's Cross had the number three bus going past it and it's an easier walk – from the north side you could come down Shandon Street, up Evergreen and you're there. Flower Lodge, the Boreenmanna Road is a long, long walk.

'Like walking down to the Páirc Uí Chaoimh. I worked down there for thirty-seven years and I hated the walk.'

What made the eventual loss of soccer to Flower Lodge all the more piercing was how striking the pitch had looked just before it shut down.

'When Liverpool came to Cork in 1987 with their league champions, Flower Lodge looked unbelievable. World class. They had brought in Bob O'Keeffe, the groundsman, and he'd been working on it for a month to get it ready for that one match, and it looked spectacular. Manicured. It looked like Wembley.

'Liverpool were double-winning champions, brought over the two cups, there was a big crowd, the kids who came along had great crack ... so it looked fantastic, as a once-off occasion.

'And because of that game, and how well it looked, that added to the whole amount of upset when it was sold, that sense of "look what we've lost out on, look what's gone."

'There was massive anger as a result, partly based, I think, on the fact that the funds to purchase it originally, in the forties, had been raised by public subscription. It was a great surface, in fairness. It was bought in 1948 but they didn't play a game on it for eight years. They spent that time getting the pitch right, but they certainly got it right.

'I went along to that first game, and you literally walked off the street on to the embankment. The AOH, who were Cork Hibernians at that stage, were playing Sligo in the FAI Cup, and it was probably the only modern FAI Cup tie played on an unenclosed pitch. A dog ran into the ground and onto the field the same day.'

Come 1987 and the Ancient Order of Hibernians – the owners of the ground – were in the mood to get rid of the asset. They were much criticised after the sale but Carter points out that they were tired of dealing with various Cork League of Ireland teams and with the FAI. The timing did not help, either; it was maybe a year too soon for the FAI, for instance.

'It was well known that it was going to be sold – it was all over the *Evening Echo* for about three months beforehand – and at the time I was told that Cork City had made a bid to buy it, but that it wasn't acceptable as an offer under Cork City's name, because they had nothing as collateral.

'The suggestion was that if Pat O'Donovan, who was involved with Cork City, had made the bid under his own name the AOH would have sold the ground to him, but there was no way they could have sold it to City, who were broke as a club. The GAA then came in, but people don't realise that the AOH were sour enough with the FAI. They felt the FAI should have done more to secure Flower Lodge, but at the time things were desperate in Dublin. Shamrock Rovers had left Glenmalure Park, Milltown, in 1987, attendances were down, the Charlton era was a year or two away from really taking off, Dalymount Park had to be refurbished …

'If Flower Lodge had gone on sale a couple of years later, there's every chance the FAI would have been able to buy it; the circumstances would have been very different.

'The other side of that, though, is it could also have become a millstone around the neck of the FAI, which is probably what would have happened if City had managed to buy it. One of their officials said to me later that it was a good thing they didn't buy it or they'd have been out of football. The crowds weren't going to Flower Lodge.'

The Cork County Board of the GAA were not the only sports organisation involved, either.

'When Cork City were in the hunt, trying to buy the stadium, the AOH got sick of them at one particular stage and offered the pitch to Cork Constitution, who were their neighbours – but Constitution turned them down.'

The Cork County Board themselves were not long out of financial danger themselves at that point. Only a decade earlier they had built Páirc Uí Chaoimh, and long-standing secretary Frank Murphy would remember the 1980s as a time when the GAA in Cork was under significant pressure.

'From February to June 1976, the year the stadium reopened, the board engaged in major bank borrowing at an interest rate of 12¾ per cent. But within three years, the rate had jumped to 20 per cent, resulting in an extra £18,000 in charges,' he told the *Irish Examiner* in 2016,

'It was a chastening time. You had to be careful with your money. That was the great lesson from the 1976 redevelopment. It was scary stuff, a matter of survival. Essentially, we weren't viable.

'We paid very close on £900,000 on interest alone. There was major concern about the possibility we were no longer viable.'

'We weren't solvent at one point. In one instance our bank interest commitment for the year exceeded our entire income from our county championships by £35,000. In 1980 alone, the amount of interest to the bank was £170,995.'

The Oliver Barry-run music festival, Siamsa Cois Laoi, would prove invaluable in reining in the Board's debts, but one particular music icon made the difference for Flower Lodge: 'The Michael Jackson concerts enabled us to buy Flower Lodge without bank borrowing,' said Murphy. 'That was huge.'

The mechanics of the bid meant it came as a surprise to the wider public.

'When it came on the market, it was on the basis that preference would be given to its retention for sport – but it was open for sport or redevelopment,' Murphy added.

'We didn't go directly or first hand, it was all done through legal representatives. We actually made two bids – one on the basis of retention for sport, and one without such a guarantee. We weren't sure what direction the vendors would take it.

'It wasn't obvious to the AOH that it was the one entity making the two offers. One was lower, the other higher – the latter on the basis of no undertaking for the retention for sport. And it was the lower one that was accepted.

'Our supposition at the time was they thought it was a soccer bid – because there was an attempt made at the time to find out who the bidders were. We had three sets of solicitors involved in total.'

Carter says the reaction of the AOH belied the GAA's caution, however: 'Then an acceptable bid came in, and they should have known it was from another organisation, and sure what other organisation was around? It had to be the GAA – who else?

'Supposedly when the bid was announced in the AOH meeting, and accepted, everyone clapped, and they said themselves at the meeting they were glad the GAA had bought it.

'They were sick of dealing with City, sick of the football fraternity, and the venue itself had gone down. The decline was rapid. At the end the average was 2,000 per week – for a team that was doing well, too.'

Still, Cork City had restored League of Ireland play to the city. It wasn't the only green shoot, either.

24

How Cork RTC Landed That Multinational

Cork RTC did not have the same lineage as UCC at first glance, but the Royal Cork Institution, going back to 1807, provided a basis for technical education in the city, and the Crawford Technical Institute took up the mantle in time.

Larry Poland joined the Crawford in September 1961, to teach electrical engineering. Within weeks of starting he was at a prize-giving ceremony in the Crawford, with politicians and officials present, and the chief inspector of the Department of Education for the Munster area told those present the time had come for Cork to have a new technical college.

'That was October 1961,' says Poland. 'We got it in 1974.'

There was also a major conference held in Cork in 1962 – Stephen P. Roche of the Crawford was a key organiser – which was focused on a college of technology for Cork and in the mid 1960s T. K. Whitaker issued reports on industrialisation, with the result that there was a push to set up technical education.

Local issues were often the main stumbling block, says Poland: 'In Dublin they had a great CEO who allowed the system to develop, while in Cork there was a focus on keeping costs down and so on.

'At that time I couldn't make a long-distance phone call to Dublin from my office. I didn't have a phone in the office for one thing, I had to walk 150 paces to use another phone, whereas the guys in Dublin could make a local call to others in Dublin. We were being held back in Cork.

'We thought we might have the college where the Regional Hospital was built, but it was felt it was too small for playing pitches and so on – there isn't room enough for cars there now – while there were also suggestions that Ballyphehane would be used, where Coláiste Stiofáin Naofa is now. The suggestion included going on both sides of the road, though, with the road going through the middle, so they didn't go for that. We ended up, then, out in Bishopstown.

'I got called Mr Electronics but that was just because I knew the companies working in that area, and I was often brought in to meet them. We didn't win them all, either, and some you knew you weren't going to get – they were just going through the motions, it was obvious.'

In the mid 1960s Poland got interested in computers and got access to a computer in the Sunbeam: 'We taught engineers a computer course – which made UCC furious: "what were we doing with computers" – but we carried on.

'At around the same time, or maybe just after, a steering committee in the Department of Education recommended establishing six regional colleges – a name we didn't like, we wanted colleges of technology as a name. Dublin VEC had designated itself colleges of technology in Bolton Street and Kevin Street.'

Significantly, Poland's interest in computers – and combining that with educating engineers – led him to create, in 1969, the first undergraduate computer engineering course: 'There was some postgrad exposure for engineering students in UCD but we were so new we had to use City & Guilds qualifications until the National Council for Educational Awards was established. When we submitted the course to them their external panel said we shouldn't be offering it, that it was too specialised.'

Being on the leading edge of technological education was recognised by others in the field, even if Cork did not always benefit. Poland can recall a manpower-forecasting seminar held in the RTC in Cork by the IDA in 1979.

'By then we were being visited by Digital Electrical Corporation, DEC, which had opened a factory in Galway earlier in the 1970s. We were furious they hadn't opened it in Cork where we had courses that would have suited them, but we didn't get them, though we were pushing our courses.

'Anyway, one of the speakers at this seminar was the HR man from DEC Galway. He stopped in the middle of his paper and looked out at me and said, "There's at least one person in the audience who knows what I'm going to say – only for the Crawford in the early 1970s, there would be no DEC in Galway."

'They were taking a lot of our graduates up there, because at the time we were the only ones teaching those courses. But Louie O'Halloran, who came up with that course, deserves the credit, not me. He produced the engineering people at undergraduate at level – he was brilliant at Boolean algebra, logic and communicating the structures.

'When DEC closed, eventually, a lot of them went on to become managers in other companies. One of them, Rob Short, eventually became a VP in Microsoft; another guy, Michael O'Sullivan, did very well also. Liam Brady became a plant manager for EMC in Massachusetts.'

The calibre of the education – and the graduates – was not an issue. But getting companies to settle in Cork was. Then Poland got a visit in the RTC, the same year that the IDA held their seminar in the college.

It was around Easter and Poland was on his own in the lab one afternoon when two men came in.

'One was in a suit – I recognised him, he was working for the IDA in Cork,' he says. 'The other one was in a check shirt, open-necked, jeans, cowboy-type boots, a huge brass buckle on his belt. No jacket, no suit. 'I was a little taken aback, but the guy in the suit introduced the other chap as Roy Mollard of Apple.

'I'd heard of Apple, though not much, but I gave them the information on what the students did, what they were capable of, and they seemed happy enough. Mollard asked a few questions and so on, and after about an hour they left.

'Next I heard Apple were opening that September. I didn't know that they were planning to come to Cork – or that the deal had been signed, sealed and delivered at that point. Early on they were working out of Alex Wrafter's mother's house somewhere in Glounthaune.

'That was the start, they grew from there. We were soon sending most of our engineering technicians up to Apple. Without them there wouldn't have been an Apple in Cork, and we didn't say that – John Twomey, who was head of engineering there said it: if it weren't for our engineering students there wouldn't have been an Apple in Cork.'

Poland did not stop there. Though there was not much industry coming in during the 1970s, 'in electronics there was always something happening,' he recalls.

'Even in the late 1980s the IDA told me they were forecasting a need for 6,000 people in the electronics industry, so I had to make a case for more students being taken on to handle that. And as it happened, the reality outstripped the IDA's prediction.'

In November 1984 he and Denis McCarthy of the IDA decided to get the companies in the area to push Cork.

'We had a meeting and decided to form the Cork Electronics Industry Association [CEIA], with companies represented by their CEOs and four cabinet members, if you like – from CIT, UCC, the IDA and FÁS, or AnCo as it was then. I wrote up the constitution and we got it going, and it's still going.

'It has been eclipsed a bit by IT@Cork, and we probably should have gone in that direction ourselves, but we were focused on manufacturing. But the fact that IT@Cork was founded by indigenous Cork companies was good, certainly.

'I chaired the small industries committee of the CEIA and one thing we did was introduce a survey to ensure that these companies, a lot of them American, were buying from local businesses. Every employee in those big industries was generating 1.5 employees outside.

'So I devised a form with columns for the companies to fill in, from left to right, headed "Imported from America", "Bought from Europe", "Bought in Ireland" and "Bought in Cork". I got them to fill those in and said I wanted to see a movement to the far right, so that they'd be buying more in Cork.

'In fairness, they committed to it and they were interested. At one stage Ben Wrafter, Alex's brother, was producing computer cabinets up in north Cork. But Apple eventually skewed the whole thing. Their numbers were so huge they could barely be analysed, so they were going places, which was great. I had to leave those out because they were swamping everything.

'It was about self-help, and about persuading prospective companies that Cork was the place to go to. It wasn't a cartel or a collection of HR people keeping salaries down.'

Poland himself got the chance to put his powers of persuasion to the test later in the decade.

By the 1980s the IDA had become much better, he says: 'For instance, they wanted everything to be completely confidential, which wasn't surprising: all those kinds of negotiations were sensitive enough and if the papers got hold of that information they'd be furious, the company might decide to leave and so on.

'The IDA knew I'd be confidential, so they were in touch with me about a company they were talking to. A couple of IDA guys from Dublin and one from Cork were bringing these guys from the company around Cork. They'd already been in Britain, Scotland and England, and they were looking at Cork next.'

Poland had a specific modus operandi when it came to industrialists casting an eye over Cork.

'I was waiting for them in the boardroom in Cork RTC, as it was then, and I did what I always did. Any time I knew there were visitors coming I'd make it a point of not allowing them to wait – I'd be sure to go out and meet them and welcome them. And when the meeting finished I'd walk them out to the car afterwards.

'Anyway, they came, I met them, and I outlined what we were doing with the students at the time. I didn't know a lot about the company, EMC, or the product – I knew what it was but it wasn't really my line. They were producing what were then called club-compatible memory boards for IBM computers. About eighteen by twelve inches, a lot of memory, faster and better than IBM's own product – that was a company that tended to be conservative, to move pretty slowly, whereas newer companies could move quicker.

'They were based in Massachusetts and I met the boss, Dick Egan, and his financial controller, who was his brother-in-law. Dick was a former Marine who'd done an engineering degree when he left the armed forces: a tough-enough nut.'

Egan and his brother-in-law appeared fairly happy with Poland's presentation but were not about to tell him there and then what their decision would be, despite the academic pushing for an answer.

'I'd always ask them – "you need to tell me what to do because I need to plan for the engineers and technicians to be ready for you when you need them," all of that. So I'd press them.

'The IDA didn't like that, but even though I didn't press them that much, I had a reason for doing so. And even if I wouldn't get the information I wanted, at least they knew I meant business.

'Anyway, when we finished, I walked them out to the car. When Dick was getting into the car, I shook his hand and said to him, "Mr Egan, if there's anything we can do to get you to decide in favour of Cork, we'll do it, even if it means changing our courses."'

Poland had spotted something: a gap in the courses, even as he was talking to the EMC executives in the college boardroom: 'We weren't doing a subject called databases on our engineering course. They wanted engineering people with some knowledge of databases, but I wasn't about to tell him the inadequacy in our course. I was willing to make that change, though.

'Egan said, "OK," and got into the back of the car and headed off. A few weeks later we heard EMC was coming to Cork, and we were delighted, of course.'

When the official opening was scheduled, Egan was invited to the ceremony in Ovens.

'It was a small affair, there were only twenty or thirty people working there then, and when I drove out to it I was met by two of my former students.

'They said hello and that Mr Egan had told them to meet me when I arrived; one of them said he'd stay with me while the other went off to find Egan. Looking back now, he probably couldn't remember what I looked like, but with the student with him he came over – "Larry, great to see you again," and we exchanged pleasantries.

'"I'm going to be off with this opening and so on for the next while," he said, "but I wanted to see you before I got started. We had a meal last night, all the employees together, and I made a statement at that meal: Larry Poland is the reason we're in Cork."

'I asked why he'd said that, and he said: "You spoke to us in the boardroom, and that was fine, you seemed happy in the college and so on, but do you remember what you said when you walked us out to the car?"

'And I did. What I learned later was that Egan's style of management and attitude to education was based on flexibility – the ability to change, and to change quickly. When he became US Ambassador to Ireland later he mentioned it again – to Mary McAleese, in newspaper reports and so on.

'Because of that I've met people who've thanked me for the jobs their children got in EMC.'

25

The Education Ecosystem

Many people have stressed the importance of education as a key element for the city: to attract people and industry, to create employment, to enhance the reputation of the entire area.

So much for the headlines. What about the fine print? How does an institution identified by one of its former heads as aloof in one of the city's greatest crises become more integrated into the community? How does another institution overcome early resistance to its programmes to drive entrepreneurship in the city? And how do they combine to greater effect?

Barry O'Connor is President of CIT and emphasises integration early on in the conversation – not just in the community, but between the IT and UCC.

'There's a lot of work being done in terms of integrating into the community – not just getting kids into third level, be it CIT or UCC, but you have learning neighbourhoods, the Lifelong Learning Festival, which is strongly supported by CIT – UCC get involved as well.

'It's about getting the whole idea of education out there. In Cork we have three of the top five FE [further education] colleges in Ireland, including the biggest, the College of Commerce. We have strong links with the College of Commerce.

'Education should be a continuum rather than "you need to get in here or there for third level"; in fact, getting to third level doesn't have to be the be-all and end-all either.'

For those it suits, third-level education is different in Cork, he says.

'I have to say that the link between UCC and CIT is unique. We have degrees jointly awarded by the two institutions – a biomedical science bachelor's, architecture bachelor's and master's, the master's in education in art and design down in the Crawford, and a BSc in industrial physics which started this year.

'No other two institutions in the country do joint awards.'

Why not?

'It's hard. It's awkward. There's a huge divide, the old binary divide between the old fashioned "tech" and the university.

'But if you have mutual respect between those involved … Take the honours degree in industrial physics: we would have strong links with the companies down the harbour, in pharma and so on, while UCC would always have had a very strong physics department. But they tended to focus on theoretical physics, teaching and so on.

'Our guys were trained as engineers with a physics background to work in industry – to look at automation and so on.

'So putting those together was going to create a stronger offering than had been there before. We're not competing with each other.'

Echoing Gerry Wrixon's comments, O'Connor points out that the co-operation extends into engineering and associated fields: 'There was a need for an architecture degree in Cork, it was felt. There's one in UL, in WIT, UCD, Bolton Street, so the thinking was there was a need for an architecture degree in Cork.

'The civil engineering degree in UCC is more broad-based – they'll do water, roads, materials, soil, fire and so on. Out here we had a very strong structural engineering degree – beams, design and so on. The two of those were combined, and we already had an architecture course which was interior architecture and architectural technology, the old-fashioned draughtsman.

'But the ingredient we also had in Cork was the Crawford, because architecture is also about aesthetics, obviously. We had that, so putting all that together allowed us to put together an architecture degree that wasn't available anywhere else. That would go into the old South Pres building. So you see there the local ingredients available which could put together a new product.'

When industry needs change, so does the offering from the colleges.

'Take biomedical science,' says O'Connor. 'There was a need for medical laboratory consultants, what used to be the med-lab techs, and they're working with hi-tech stuff, so there were guys in UCC stronger on the science side and guys in CIT stronger on the analytical side.

'That degree was decided by the staff coming together and agreeing they could do a different degree – it was mainly microbiology in UCC and biological sciences here, so you had two different sides.

'That was how the tech was done down long ago – "they're more practical". What it was really was, though, was that they were professional. I found when I came to CIT was that guys were super-strong on the theory here also, but they could also put that into practice. In the road [UCC], it's more academic, more emphasis on the theory.'

The ultimate endorsement of that co-operation is visible on the very degrees awarded, he says.

'Five or six years ago the government decided to rationalise the number of colleges producing teachers and in the case of Cork we were brought in with UCC and were told we wouldn't be giving degrees in education any more.

'We sat down together and worked out the PME, the Professional Master's in Education – the arts side was in the Crawford and the practical teaching side was in UCC. The parchment for those has a UCC badge and a CIT badge.

'There's an NUI badge because UCC are tied in with them, but they're unique, having the badges of different colleges on them.'

John O'Halloran, Deputy President and Registrar in UCC, agrees with O'Connor about the two institutions being 'in an education ecosystem'. He sees a deep integration of third-level learning in the city, a major change since the 1980s.

'I think most people would accept that UCC and CIT have the best relationship of any institute of technology and university in the sector. We're student-focused, and there are those degrees we award together.

'Then there's how we connect to the city through the Learning City and UNESCO project – and economically: every student generates three to four jobs' worth of revenue in the city. But the Learning City and UNESCO project, that's putting Cork on a global stage, it's not just that this is great in Ireland, it's far wider.

'And that goes a long way back, the commitment to lifelong learning goes back as far as seventy years, when Alfred O'Rahilly of UCC brought in the first lifelong learning programmes. Add in the fact that that's penetrated to UCC and CIT and also the Education and Training Board, the City Council, which is something you wouldn't necessarily have predicted a few years ago.

'There are different lenses involved – learning through the workplace, the school, the university, the library. That's all changed since the 1980s, when you went to the campus and someone gave a class, and that was that. Nowadays there's a sense of connectivity. What we're doing now is the connected curriculum, connecting that to the real life of the city – the city in Ireland, the city in the world.

'The green agenda is another aspect of that. Not only is that a big global issue, but we find that young people really want to engage in matters like that, so the city derives a benefit from that. Cork University Hospital is part of our teaching ecosystem, and it's the first hospital in the world to be awarded the "Green Fag" for its efforts in reducing its carbon footprint: there's a ripple going out into the community.

'And coming back in, because every time students go out and learn they bring that back into the university also. I'd say there have been enormous changes for the betterment of everybody.'

The commitment of specific individuals is always helpful, as Barry O'Connor points out.

'First of all, there's great synergy between CIT and UCC, particularly on the science side. There's respect between the two. Gerry Wrixon would be a good example of that, he's someone who always had great time for the people out here.

'When he became President of UCC there was a meeting in the Civil Engineering building in UCC and Paddy Murphy asked Gerry, "President, are we going to have a mechanical engineering degree?"

'Gerry said, "There's a fine mechanical engineering out the road. Answer: no."

227

'There was great respect on the engineering and science side, certainly, and knowing each other helped absolutely.'

John O'Halloran agrees. 'Leadership makes a difference. The likes of Barry O'Connor, Michael Murphy, Padraig Ó Sé, myself, Ted Owens in the ETB, Ann Doherty, Ciaran Lynch, Tina Neylon – all those people working together with the Learning Festival, for instance, meant 600 people came from all over the world to see it.

'There's no learning festival in the States, for instance. San Francisco was very interested in doing so, as was the University of Massachusetts in Lowell. They're having an event along those lines this year.'

O'Halloran runs the Quercus programme for talented students in UCC, and individual relationships were key to a recent development on that front also, one which involved a familiar name.

'The Quercus programme is about capturing and retaining talented students, and recognising that talent in a different way – that they're not only good academically but they might be good at sport, music and so on.

'Ford had that 100-year anniversary in Cork recently and they came on board to sponsor the programme for five years. That has been terrific in terms of profile, connections, opportunities for students – that has all exploded.

'And that was because Ford was here in Cork, the contribution to Cork and from Cork. William Clayton Ford was here and was very much taken by Cork – and Ballinascarthy – and at one point he said the students in Cork were as good as anywhere in the world. Pretty good affirmation from a Princeton man.

'So that looks back a hundred years but also looks forward to a time when there may be driverless cars in Cork, a whole other level of technology.'

Within the city, UCC in particular has changed. When O'Halloran refers to 4,000 students coming to Cork from overseas, he points out that when those students go back, they push the city in their home places.

'I remember being in Shanghai recently enough, talking to UCC alumni who were all Chinese, and also to prospective students. What I noticed, though, was that the conversation moved on to where in Cork the prospective students could get authentic ingredients for their Chinese meals.

'That's real. And I was really proud of the university and the city, to hear that in Shanghai. A couple of days ago I had a conversation about a sustainability project from my office with people in Columbia, Mexico, North America, Cork city and west Cork. We have a global reach on a daily basis which has been enabled by technology, so that has really changed from the 1980s also.

'How does it work? The community, the society and industry need people, so institutions like ours are educating people for all of those. Equally there's the research and innovation side – and we're the highest research income university in the country – and outputs are important. The connections with fintech, pharma, biomedical and technology industries are all very important in that regard, they're all interested in having high-quality people. They're also interested in ideas, the incubation of ideas – some of those fail but others take off.'

There is a quantifiable aspect to the notion that Cork is somewhere special when it comes to innovation. O'Halloran has been judging the BT Young Scientist competition for eighteen years and is often asked why so many winners of the competition have come from Cork.

'It's not just a matter of one school, or one teacher in one school – several schools have good records in the competition:

Kinsale, Scoil Choilm, Coláiste Treasa, Crosshaven. First off, 20 per cent of the entrants come from Cork and the greater Cork area. That's quite disproportionate, but Cork is also higher when it comes to getting CAO points for science, technology, engineering and maths.

'What we have, I think, is a science capital with industry, UCC, CIT and a commitment to learning. That makes it attractive and drives the whole thing – you're a university graduate so you want your kids to be graduates, people coming in from the outside want quality … there's a honeypot effect driving a demand for higher quality.'

Barry O'Connor feels more foreign students could come to Cork, given the suitability of the city for those new to Ireland.

'One huge opportunity we're not making enough use of is the foreign student market, particularly given the size of Cork – or the smallness of Cork.

'You couldn't beat Cork as a venue for students. Cork is compact, relatively safe, has a huge educational infrastructure. I think, as a city, Cork could do more to bring them in and look after them; it's not Dublin, so they won't get lost here.

'There are targeted areas but there are also opportunities. Last summer we had the International Space University here, for instance.'

The ISU is a movable feast – a 'neutral international forum' is how it describes itself – a mobile learning hub teaching about space, which meant 125 full-time students were in CIT for the whole summer, 30-odd full-time staff from the Space University, 'and a couple of hundred professors from Harvard, MIT,' says O'Connor.

'They've been all over the world with this Space University, but Cork is the only place they've wanted to come back to. They asked if they could come back here because of the experience they had.'

Little things helped, he adds. The Rising Sons Brewery in the Coal Quay produced two beers specially for the ISU: first, One Small Step beer and then, at the end of their stay, One Giant Leap beer. Keary's Motor Group lent the ISU a car while it was here. They specifically mentioned the ladies in the canteen who'd been so good to them,' says O'Connor.

'While they were here, then, they got involved with the Midsummer Festival, with Blackrock Castle, they were all staying in Diggins Hall.

'If it's marketed properly, Cork could do very well. We were lucky that Niall Smith, our head of research, is big into that, he and Liz Kerley, they took it on and the place was buzzing for the summer.

'It's not like people are working against each other, but if we worked together like that just a bit more, it'd help.'

26

Learning from the Past

Both O'Halloran and O'Connor stress the need to take on the lessons of the past when looking to the future. The departure of the big industries of the 1980s, for instance, was not followed by an outburst of entrepreneurship; it didn't exist in the culture to the same extent then. Barry O'Connor says CIT tries to drive enterprise across its courses.

'There's always a danger with large companies that they may move on,' says O'Connor.

'That happened with Ford and Dunlop and when that happens it causes consternation, obviously enough.

'I remember someone from the IDA saying to me that when Ford and Dunlop closed, only two entrepreneurial ventures came out of it when all the lads got their redundancy packages. The notion wasn't there, that you could take a chance on something, a venture.

'That entrepreneurial spirit is being driven. We have a centre for entrepreneurship and we try to include an entrepreneurial element in our courses. Even with the big companies, from Ford to Apple, there are usually smaller businesses feeding into those, and the changes that those big companies go through.

'Take the Idaho potato: the potato farmers in that part of the States were making a fortune out of that crop but felt, maybe with reason, that they mightn't always make that kind of money out of potatoes, so they looked around for an alternative, and ended up putting their money into fibre-optics. With the result that there's a huge fibre-optic research facility in Idaho now – paid for by the potato.'

O'Connor points to the CIT engineering exhibition for the Cork version of the Idaho spirit.

'CIT is the single biggest engineering school on the island of Ireland, and every March there's an engineering exhibition, the biggest in the country.

'Every engineering student – and there are hundreds of them – has to come up with a product. Road barriers, new methods for baling hay, all of that. It's not engineering for the sake of engineering, it's coming up with a product, one that works.

'Ten years ago a couple of students came up with an idea for a kind of ski boot for a horse, because obviously if a horse breaks a leg it has to be put down, it can't put weight on its hoof. With their boot, though, it could survive, and they won awards all over Europe with it.

'Another couple of students devised a test for hurling helmet visors; a Chinese student who was here came up with a mechanism for a hospital drip that would prevent bubbles forming in the drip, because a bubble in your drip is fatal.

'Two more lads joined up with James Harty, the orthopaedic surgeon, to come up with a protective covering for people who suffer a fracture of the small finger: that was serious engineering design. A detector to prevent cot death in babies, another one.'

Not every idea is a winner, but the trick is to train students to come up with ideas in the first place.

'When you get kids thinking along those lines you get products that can be developed, and there might be two jobs in it, or five jobs, or twenty. If you get them to think outside the box, then they'll come up with these things.

'Every first-year student here does a CIT module: creativity, innovation and teamwork. It's about getting them to think about what they want to do and to work with other people.

'It's important that the business side of the house works with the engineers, say, because the engineer can come up with a design, but if the marketing guy says "that won't sell", well ...

'It encourages the students to think about what will work. The key thing is here that we identify problems and look for solutions to those problems; we don't develop solutions and then look for problems to solve.'

Sometimes when the idea works it is demonstrably more cost-efficient than similar projects.

'Munster Rugby were based over in the Tyco building for a few years and one of our students put sensors on the scrum machine to measure the forces the lads were putting on it. After a session on the scrum machine, Rob Penney, then the coach, would put them through the mill in the gym and send them back to the scrum machine to see how they'd do then. And the sensors would measure how well they were doing.

'The comparison was with Toulouse, who had a similar machine built for them by Airbus or one of the big tech companies in the city. That cost €200,000 while the students here did it for a couple of grand. They didn't even need it to be completely hi-tech either. They also developed a platform for line-outs. Normally you need two or three lads to lift the jumper, but the students worked up an aluminium rig to lift the jumper instead.'

There are concerns. There always are. Funding is a constant, buzzing headache for third-level institutions.

'What doesn't help is that we don't get funding for research,' says O'Connor. 'And research in engineering is expensive. There was a system agreed where an institute of technology would get a grant of €1,000 from the government for a business student, someone who just sat at a desk, while that rose to €1,700 for engineering students because you had to buy equipment and chemicals and so forth. There were different categories for funding.

'That was fine when the government paid it but when everyone started paying the €3,000 contribution and the government paid the balance, that balance came with a multiplier.

'So we – all the colleges and universities – are getting less money for research for engineers, though we're doing exactly what the government wants in terms of co-operating with business and looking at the needs of industry.'

John O'Halloran takes the idea of challenging students and gives it another twist: to create adaptable people.

'The principal of Our Lady of Lourdes school said something to me once which stuck with me – "You can't educate a hungry child." And you can't educate an unhealthy child either.

'We've pushed the idea of not just lifelong learning but life-wide learning, to support students in other aspects of their lives – to be creative, to work in teams, to provide leadership. It's believed now that your children will change jobs at least six times in their lifetimes, when your father and my father probably did one job for most of their lives.

'We need to support children to be resilient – and to be proficient in IT and digital skills, which are two areas to work on. The university's a very different place now.

'People you're talking to – and people I'm talking to – might have absorbed that, the need to be adaptable. But has everybody? Those that haven't adapted may be left behind, which isn't great; an educational institution should be helping everyone to become adaptable.

'The other side is whether young people want to be in the one place for their entire lives, whether they even aspire to the notion of a "job for life" when they're interested in change, in travel, in all of those things. The challenge then comes in how people invest in their own futures – how does that new connectivity work there, or not? I don't know.'

Connectivity and digital skills are areas that were only emerging ten years ago; in the 1980s they were the preserve of science fiction. But both CIT and UCC are in the business of anticipating future needs with planning their courses years in advance. How is that done in the broadest sense and in the narrowest sense, i.e., how do those courses suit Cork and its needs?

'If we're developing a new programme,' says O'Connor, 'and this is how it impacts on the city, the first thing the guys proposing it have to do is produce a feasibility study.

'That means, basically, is there a need for the programme? Will there be jobs for the people who do this course? We don't make any apologies for that. In UCC the attitude would be different, you can dream up a course and get published in journals on it and so on, but we start by asking if there are jobs available.

'There's a downside to that as well, though. Our graduates get jobs, which is great, but the other side is that they don't hang around to do research – but the work is done if they get jobs, and anyway there are other ways to get them to do a master's while they're working. For the feasibility studies, fellas have to produce evidence, it's not just "ah there'll be forty engineers needed in

Cork next year." You have to prove it, and if you can't, then it doesn't move.'

There are concrete examples of how courses develop and expand, he adds: 'EMC are a good example, because they came to Cork originally because of Larry Poland, who taught here, but also because when they came to Cork first they needed their workers trained up, so they came to CIT, or the RTC as it was then.

'As the processes became more complicated they asked if the RTC could train their staff to become technicians, so they came up with an accelerated technician programme, a one-year programme. That meant lads who'd been on the factory floor became technicians – and as time moved on again they needed to get degrees, so we developed a degree course for them.

'And three or four years ago that moved on again, with cloud computing becoming an area for EMC, so EMC then came back to us, meaning that lads who'd been on the factory floor, who'd become technicians and then picked up degrees, they needed to be trained again – so between us and EMC we came up with the first cloud-computing degree in the world, and it's been sold online all over the world.

'That's the co-operation. We work with Teagasc and others, but that's a classic example, the EMC case. They came in, we came up with something, then they upped their game, as always happens in these cases and we had to come up with a higher level of training. That's the direct involvement of business and locality.'

Isn't predicting developments in cutting-edge technology difficult, if not impossible?

'That's what you should be doing in a third-level institution. There's a lot of talk about responding to the needs of industry, but across there in the Nimbus building we have fifty people working on electronics research. Apart from the good research they're doing, which is valuable in itself, they're also working on trying to identify the trends which are coming down the tracks. If you're training kids to be engineers, or in technology generally, and you're starting them off this year, they won't be out for another four years, so you need to be able to tell them, "here are three possible avenues for you to go with your qualification."

'When the time comes maybe one of those will be a dead end, but a couple of them might be winners, and at least they come out with a sense of what's happening. We have to try to build that into the courses so the students have some idea of where to go.

'We bring in €16 million a year for research, which would be chicken feed compared to UCC, but we have a different mission, and we're not funded for research the way universities are. Every student that goes into university, the government gives a piece of money to the university for research. We just get money to teach, so we have to scrimp and find money for research.'

John O'Halloran takes the notion of courses suited to a local constituency and directs it outwards.

'Think of a small company in west Cork: its global reach is probably quite limited. Then consider a market with one eighth of the world's population: China. Now, there may be a market opportunity there for that company, but consider also that if a Chinese student comes to Cork to study and then goes to work at that company, suddenly there's a connection back to China.

'China is becoming important, but so are India and South America – the conversation I had with people in Columbia related to the peace process in that country, and the FARC rebels. We were talking about land use, and changing cocaine crops to alternative crops …

'The Columbians are tied in with the Northern Ireland peace process, so they're coming here later this year to discuss that.'

O'Halloran says the diversity among the student body – another change from the 1980s – has impacted on course content in UCC.

'We have offices in Shanghai, New York and Mumbai and they're recruiting students. We have those 4,000 foreign students, so it's significant. People focus on the money aspect of that, and it's important, but it's also about cultural awareness – SAT scores rise when people are exposed to a range of different creativities.

'One of the challenges for us as a society is dealing with that, so we run a module on cultural awareness – greetings, all of that. Take the red and white of Cork – it'd be great for Chinese people, who love red, but maybe not so much for Arab cultures.

'That module – about behaviours – can only be good. It's a positive side of globalisation. People talk about the democratisation of education, and we have 600 students online across the country – that's the other new way, students who won't set foot in the university, literally, until they graduate. It's good in that it's flexible, bad in the sense they don't get the immersive campus experience, all the diversity involved in that.'

Responding to that diversity with greater inclusion is another area where the modern campus differs from the 1980s.

'Equality, diversity and inclusion is the other big issue – we're a university of refuge now, of sanctuary, and we got a bronze medal in the Athena SWAN awards scheme because our policies are speaking to those values.

'Again, that's trying to be responsive and respectful, to create a society that's equally important to women and children, and for diversity. Go back to the 1980s and that diversity didn't exist – in people, in pedagogy, in technology, in employment. There are now almost as many foreign students as there were students, full stop, in the mid 1980s. It has changed that much.

'The sports infrastructure has changed, which also adds to the sense of education going beyond books.'

For all the strength of the local offering in education, O'Halloran is not blind to the international influence, pointing out that the future educational experience may be a combination of UCC with other courses from across Ireland and beyond.

'Say you want to study commerce at UCC – but there's a related course at Harvard which you're interested in. You come to me and say "I'm interested in that course too, and I want it on my transcript."

'Then there are micro-credentials. We started off doing a degree, three years or four years, but where did that come from? That's something David Putnam refers to quite a bit when he's in here with us – nano-degrees you build up in fractions. That's the lifelong aspect of it.

'Then there's the life-wide part of it, digital badges, not unlike the Scout badges idea, where we award badges for accomplishment in different areas. Those micro-credentials can go on your LinkedIn page or wherever and some universities are already using that for credit-building programmes.

'We launched those recently and when you attach them they can be opened online – you can see what they were awarded for, that it's not just a matter of ticking a box, but there's real substance to it.'

Funding is an obvious challenge for the Cork institutions going forward. O'Halloran is a fan of the 21st-century approach to learning remotely, but there's also the physical campus.

'Capital investment, infrastructure, facilities – we want the best facilities and resources and some of the buildings in UCC aren't much different to the 1980s, which isn't something you'd say with pride. That's not great, and it's a legacy of a lack of capital investment.

'There are some fantastic new buildings but we need some investment in that area so that students go into facilities which are as good as their secondary schools at the very least.

'I was in Skibbereen recently to see their new school, and it is one of the best teaching places I ever saw, but if you came from there to UCC you wouldn't be thinking, "this is a step up" in terms of facilities. We have to work on that collectively.

'The other aspect is people. When you and I were in college there were probably around 5,000, 6,000 students. Now there are 22,000 and staff numbers haven't grown accordingly – not that that growth should be linear, but we need to ensure the staff–student ratio is better.

'The other big difference between now and the 1980s is technology, obviously enough. The whole idea of blended pedagogy is strong now: rather than standing up talking to students, you give them material in advance online, they come in and you discuss it … the future university is already emerging and may look more like primary education.

'By that I mean the teacher's desk may be in the corner of the primary classroom while he or she is in the centre of the room with the children around them. University learning has also become more collaborative. There's not just knowledge – "stuff" – but you must scaffold the learning, the pedagogy is changing so much.

'We're looking for different mixes of technology – and for different people, too. Don't forget it now takes longer to become a teacher than a doctor – four years of science and two years for the equivalent of a H.Dip. compared to five years of medicine.

'So we need to keep an eye on that aspect of education, too, but those are the kinds of things that strike me about education or the university then and now.'

Barry O'Connor sees a slightly different headache on the horizon, which might impact on CIT and Cork alike: 'Mary

Moloney of CIT recently gave a talk and pointed out that all the broadband interconnectors in Ireland go into Dublin, with one exception. They managed to get one into Cork.

'But it hasn't been switched on, because a big user is needed before it can be switched on. If it were switched on, broadband in Cork would be unbelievable, and then you'd get the users coming in for it. But while they're holding on until a big user signs up for it, the cost of a broadband connection for an industry in Cork is five times what it is in Dublin.

'Would a Facebook be a big user? I don't know. It's like Jackie Healy-Rae looking for an orthodontic lab in Kerry when there were no orthodontists: he said if you had the birdcage you'd get the bird, and he was right.'

Before we met, John O'Halloran had gone to Philip King's Ireland's Edge conference, where people discuss a range of issues which have a specific impact on the periphery of the country and those who live there.

'A theme that came up was remaining competitive – take the issue of broadband, for instance. But one of his speakers was a woman running an animation company in Galway: she said she'd been in San Francisco, where a month's rent would pay a year's rent in Ireland. It's a ten-minute journey for her from home to work, so immediately cost and quality of life were big factors in favour of Ireland, as well as the creativity she saw in Irish students.

'Take Galway, Limerick, Mayo, Cork – there's an onus on us, a responsibility to create an ecosystem there, with the city as a honeypot and nodes around it. For instance, we run a module on sustainability and it's delivered into Dingle, where there are thirty people in a room – but there are also sixty-five in a room in UCC, as well as ten in a room in Skibbereen.

'So there are opportunities there for people to have rural living but also have an urban quality of life if the connectivity is there. We're really foregrounding those there across our parish – which we regard as Munster.'

O'Halloran is not the only person to point out the possibilities offered to Cork by Brexit, particularly as Dublin becomes more and more unmanageable across a range of areas.

'Brexit is an opportunity for a place like Cork because we're English-speaking, and we have a lot of significant industry already in the area. Dublin's getting congested and urbanisation is a real issue there. If we get our act together – and in education we're really working on that – it's a real opportunity.

'The speed bumps coming down the road, to me, would be a lack of urgency to put in the required infrastructure. What do I mean by that? Say we want to connect our campus to the playing fields in Bishopstown – in real terms, it's not that far but mentally it's quite far, particularly in terms of infrastructure.

'As employment starts to grow then there may be more pressure on accommodation, so on a couple of fronts I think we may be approaching a tipping point to support accommodation, to support connectivity – but to do so in a sustainable way.

'In my ideal world I'd have driverless cars, for instance, connecting different campuses. That kind of experimentation, of a modern university in the city, would be great.

'Another speed bump is our imagination, the extent to which we want to try different things. Ironically enough, a university can be conservative, given that it's trying to foster new thinking, but then again it's also a large institution and it is pulled in many different directions while trying to maintain a core of research and teaching.'

27

A Different Place Then. A Different Place Now

In 1988, Pat Fitzgerald decided to go back to Cork.

'At the back of my mind I probably always wanted to do something myself, and I was fascinated by recruitment in London – I didn't know anything about it but I couldn't believe people were paying to find fellas like me.

'I remember things being tough at home but compared to what we saw in the recent crash, I don't remember anything like that because I wasn't here and when I was here, I was in college, in that bubble where you're away from it, really.

'I probably realised at the time that there was a flow of Irish people going to London all the time so I had the idea to set up a recruitment firm in Ireland specifically to place people in London. It wasn't to place people in Ireland, as I didn't think there was any market in Ireland. 'I wanted to set up in Dublin but I didn't have enough money to do that, plus I still knew people in Cork who were coming out of college and so on, so I set up in Cork rather than Dublin.'

Getting a company off the ground is difficult in any era, whether the going is good or bad. In the 1980s it was particularly difficult, however.

'Trying to set up back then – I would say it was harder,' says Fitzgerald. 'The one thing I remember specifically was the complete lack of supports. There were start-your-own-business grants, but you had to be signing on for sixteen or twenty-four weeks before you qualified for those, which meant you had to take six months off to sign on for £70 or £80 a week in order to get the grant … I wanted to get going.

'People ask me when things changed, but for me at that time it was the first three or four years of trying to start a business, I don't know when things changed. You're just trying to do something and the market is what it is – you can't look back as you can now, from thirty years on, and say "those five years were great" or "those five years were bad."

'The quality of Irish graduates and newly qualified accountants in Ireland, though – we were working with other recruiters in Ireland; we'd find people and they'd find the jobs, and I couldn't believe how well-regarded newly qualified Irish accountants were. They'd literally get off the plane in London and there'd be five or six interviews with blue-chip employers waiting for them.

'Nowadays, they can access that themselves – it's totally different. But the change came about in the early 1990s happened when it no was longer automatic that people left for London. There were more questions asked about opportunities here, few and far between though they were.

'From the point of view of the banks, I remember trying to get money – though this was a little later than the 1980s – and we approached a couple of banks. We'd been with a small bank but wanted to move, so we went to the two main banks.

'The person we met in the first was very conservative, and couldn't understand we were asking for money without bricks and mortar to build it up. All we had was a business that was making a few bob but he couldn't get his head around it – he couldn't get his head around why we felt we could get money from them, too.

'We went across the road and met someone who was fundamentally different and looked at the project in a completely different way. I'd suspect there wasn't that much of a difference between the two banks, that we were just lucky in who we met in the second one. There are loads of options for funding for companies trying to get going now – loads of them. Back then it was very difficult.'

Given the emphasis on the job for life in the older industries, it is interesting to hear Fitzgerald trace the decay of that idea – or rather, its disappearance altogether.

'The other thing that started to change in the late 1990s was the number of times people started to change jobs. The job for life was gone.

'Into the 2000s – and still – people would ask, "why did you leave that job after two years?" I remember a time when if someone left a job after three years and it was on their CV, it was a real question mark. Now they might be gone after three months.

'I'm not saying which is right or wrong, but that has changed. And younger people now feel their careers come first, and I don't know where the balance is in what's best for the employee and what's best for the employer.'

Fitzgerald can compare the effect the recent crash had on employees with that of the 1980s.

'We probably got a flavour of that again back in 2009 to 2011. What we noticed was that, bad as the market got back then, and it was bad, the jobs that were there were good jobs with good companies – people were afraid to move. That fear had come back – the people who didn't have jobs, it was different for them, but those with jobs, who would have moved in a normal market because it would have been best for their careers, didn't move. That old sense of "better the devil I know" had come back – "where I am is reasonably stable, I'm not sure of the other place." Even though it might be a blue-chip company as an option, that fear was back.

'I often think when times are bad people look at those who don't have jobs – but we also see people who have jobs, people who are slowing down their careers because of that fear factor.'

And there are other factors. There's a more entrepeurial spirit now, he says.

'That's definitely a factor. And everything is easier, from legals to property, all of that. Go back to the 1980s and that was harder. It was very old-fashioned: we had our first office on the Grand Parade and ... I understand if you have an office to let and some young fella walks in you're wary or whatever, but I imagine that now it's a lot easier. There are plenty of incubation spaces there now which didn't exist then.

'Back then you had to take on a lease, do things you don't have to do now – there are stepping stones for a new business. That wasn't the case then.'

When things were very bad a few years ago, a friend of Fitzgerald's lost his job and said he was fearful that Cork wouldn't provide for his kids.

'Now he was down at the time, but I asked him why it had to be Cork. I'm a Kerryman, maybe it's different, but there is that thing about Cork people. I have kids and I'd love them to live in Cork. Do I expect them to live in Cork? Probably not. I hope they travel and I hope they come back, but it's a lottery.

'But there's no doubt there's a thing in Cork that you stay, never mind come back. Almost that you tough it out here. Is Cork different from that point of view? Maybe.'

It has its attractions apart from that. Fitzgerald evaluates the city.

'Young people want to go to the big cities for the fun and the opportunities and so on, and if you look at their employment histories through their twenties, you see them changing jobs every eighteen months maybe.

'But a lot of them, when they hit early to mid thirties, that period, they're beginning to think more long term. That's where Cork has an advantage.

'First, those people have experience and they've gone through ten employers by the age of thirty, they're more likely to settle, and I think there's an advantage there to tap into for Cork – to make sure the opportunities are there for them in Cork. Was it like that back in the day? I'm not sure.'

Where will they work? The great question lurking at the back of all conversations for this book is a simple one: should Cork worry about Apple and EMC?

'I'm an optimist, so no. Do I think they'll both be there in five to ten years – I don't know but I'd think it's unlikely.

'But you have to remember that a lot of the people employed there are highly skilled, highly talented people. Apple have people doing customer service, which is transient enough – people come here for a couple of years and then they move on – but there's also a very skilled labour force. It's not like Dell in Limerick, which was manufacturing, or Apple when it started off in Cork, which was a lot of manufacturing as well. A lot of the people employed there now ... it's not as easy to take on 200 to 300 engineers, because you can't get them.

'That doesn't mean those numbers can't be built up gradually in another location, but the stickiness is the workforce.

'Obviously, if you have a big bang some morning and one or the other of them pulls out, then there'd be a huge effect. But if Apple or EMC drop a thousand jobs each over the next three years, those people can be reabsorbed back into employment.

'To me, that's different. As I say, I don't remember the detail of Ford and Dunlop, but take Dell, when they pulled the jobs out of Limerick. Those were assembly jobs which could be done cheaper elsewhere, and let's be honest, when they can do what they do in Cork cheaper elsewhere, they'll do it then again.

'Unless we're ahead of that curve we'll be in trouble.'

What are the other takeaways? After the turmoil and chaos, what was learned from the darkest days of the recent past which could forearm Cork for the future?

28

'Fierce Notions': Cork's Future

'**P**rior to Ford's and Dunlop's closing, there was an order to Cork. There was a pattern to life,' says Pat Casey.

'The Ford's guys and the Dunlop's guys had good jobs, and there were plenty of other places feeding off those directly and indirectly. They had their social structures and their sporting structures, and a huge number of people rotated through that.

'Those guys came to the pub regularly, you could set your watch by them – and then it was replaced by chaos, really, because the foundations for life were gone.

'There was a pace and a regularity to life at that point. That's not to say that there weren't bad aspects to life, but there wasn't the element of surprise. You can discuss employment levels and economics and so on, but there was a feeling of dislocation after the closures, and that percolated through community and individual life.

'It was the change that was always coming, but we've come out of it pretty well.'

The change that was always coming is a good description. Theo Dorgan's view of Ireland crystallises that change: 'You know the old joke about the 1960s not happening in Ireland until the 1970s? In the 1970s you saw mobile capital operate, capital that wasn't tied to its country of origin, and at around the same time the IDA started its strategy of bringing in foreign multinationals, particularly in electronics and chemicals.

'All of that brought shocks with it, but those shocks had already been absorbed in more developed economies. By the time they got to Ireland elements of the solution were already appearing in those other economies; when Germany realised that heavy engineering wasn't a beaten docket, exactly, but that electronics and pharmaceuticals were the coming industries – well, they'd gone through the traditional industry lay-offs, and the associated shocks, and they were coming back with responses.

'Then here's the IDA locking on to that, so in a very short time we were absorbing the shock of the death of the old manufacturing economy and also gearing up for the early-twenty-first century economy. In a way, the shock period was very short because the solutions were already coming on stream.

'For instance, during a brief period in the late 1980s we had the most advanced telecommunications system in the world, because we'd had to replace – in its entirety – a completely outmoded system. That was replaced by a state of the art system: I remember going to the States around then and you'd nearly pity them, their phone system was so out of date compared to ours.

'The old model of a job for life in serious assembly-line work, that was already disappearing in advanced economies. And when they disappeared here, the solutions in those advanced economies were available for immediate translation here. But that was a mirror of the culture.'

What was the big driver of change, then?

'For me it was Apple,' says Kathleen Lynch. 'That new world – innovative, tech-driven – coming to Cork made a huge difference. It had an employment benefit – good jobs, good money and no cultural snobbery attached. Apple also invested in the people working there.

'But there was a knock-on effect with parents of seeing the benefit of education, the importance of investing in education. Those parents saw a wage coming into the house and they saw there was a benefit to the education.'

Joe Tuohy was there to see the culture shift and echoes Lynch, particularly about Apple.

'When I came to Cork there was Ford's, Dunlop's and Goulding's, and they were the dominant presences at any Chamber of Commerce functions you went to, for instance.

'I was invited up to speak to the Chamber one time about the dockyard and it was full of guys from those places, and there was a culture that time, probably, of fellas going for long lunches and maybe heading back to the office for an hour in the afternoon. Those were sunset industries but they dominated the Chamber, the IMI, all of those. What transformed Cork, to me, was Apple. We got involved – with Project Management – a bit with Apple and in those early days a few things struck me. How young everybody was, and how informal the place was. And how many women were running meetings, for instance. I'd never seen a woman run a meeting, for instance, until I went up to Apple.

'And the managing director's office was visible to everyone, so you could see if he was reading the paper or scratching his head or drinking coffee. Even getting taxis to the airport. They must have transformed the taxi industry in Cork, but they were transformational in a lot of other ways as well.'

Pat Casey endorses that sense of a shift in influences within the city.

'The "merchant princes" thing is overdone, but there's no doubt that there were families and businesses which were massively influential in the city for many, many years. The upheaval and closures of the 1980s also served to bring in other people like Gerry Wrixon and Owen O'Callaghan.

'It's interesting that the Chamber, a pretty conservative institution, began to reflect those changes. There were new faces there and it no longer became the province of half a dozen families and the main banks. You had a more eclectic bunch of people emerging, and it's unrecognisable now compared to what it was before.

'The Chamber and the Cork Business Association were giving more solid critiques, too. Analysis is more empirical now, but I feel now, still, that the *Examiner*'s fixation for years with the unfairness of it all wasn't particularly helpful. There wasn't enough "where are we going?"'

'When alternative enterprises were being set up, the cumulative message was that there was now a new generation in business. I think if we'd spent less time feeling sorry for ourselves we'd have recovered quicker, but that's not to minimise the impact these closures had on people, which was huge. All their comforts had been snatched away.'

Away from industry, the city has also changed hugely. For the better, Ronnie Dorney believes.

'I think things have improved significantly for people. There was a piece done on the north side of the city by RTÉ before the 2015 election and the tone was "nothing has changed". I'd say there has been huge change. A lot of infrastructural change, a lot of programmes on the ground. I thought the programme was glib enough, and biased.

'There has been investment. You only have to see photographs of the city then and now to see that. So we've moved on.'

Socially there has been movement. Dorney herself can attest to that.

'I got married a couple of years ago, which shows that there have been advances, huge advances since then. And those advances apply in other areas as well, obviously, but a friend of mine in Limerick was saying recently someone in a class she teaches – an American – asked about the gay scene in Ireland. They were told by someone else in the class, "Dublin for the gay boys, Cork for the girls."

'There's a lesbian resource centre in Cork and I've been involved with it personally and professionally. It's good to have resources like that and there's a lot of work going on.

'So it's different, certainly. When I got married I lost count of the number of people who congratulated me, and us, and the number of those who said, "my own daughter came out a while back" or "my son is gay", so maybe seeing people get married, or even the marriage equality vote itself, it's much more positive now. There are even decent films about the experience now compared to the gloomy stuff we used to see, you'd be depressed coming out after seeing them.

'For those of us that came out back then the community was small, but it was a community. You had to be careful because there were places you didn't want to go and there were people who were attacked and beaten. It was different then to the kind of agenda we're seeing these days in Europe; it was equality, not marriage equality, back then, but if you look at one of those maps of the world that show you where it's safe to be gay or lesbian and where it's not, Ireland is one of the former.

'And part of that is down to people's generosity, too. I think Irish people are generous, genuinely, and that's been part of some of the developments of recent years – and how we've engaged in changes. The sense of doing something out of fear has been removed.'

Micheál Martin feels Cork still has challenges it hasn't quite come to terms with.

'I'd argue that the city council did a lot at the time with local area development plans, for instance. The South Parish was in my area and, looking back, the inner city was becoming denuded of people so there was a constant need to reinvent the South Parish and the Middle Parish, even if latterly you'd wonder what those rows were for – the big road through Grattan Street that was mooted never happened in the end, for example.

'It's the struggle between growing urbanisation and city life and how you make that compatible with city living. We didn't ever quite get that right in my view, and we're still struggling with it, to make city centre living compatible with having small kids, for instance.

'I think there are some incompatibilities there, you're probably better off out in the suburbs with them, but given all the tech companies in Cork now and the young people working in those, if you could get some development into apartments, making those more stylish … but the demographic has changed totally.

'The population in the South Parish was bigger then. For instance, in the local elections in 1985, there were plenty of ballot boxes in St Killian's on the Evergreen Road, but those are gone. I'd have had eleven boxes up there one time but they're gone. Turner's Cross is now about six boxes – all old Pearse Wyse territory, which became mine. You can track the population like that, and to a large extent it's gone.

'But in the 1980s the city was wrestling with that hankering for city life, city communities. Modernity, traffic, the higher intensity of a modern city, maybe, compared to the forties and fifties.'

The 1980s are long gone, though, never mind the 1940s and 1950s. What about Cork's future?

'Resilience, adaptability,' says Martin. 'Those are very important. You have to read the tea leaves and see the shifting trends and recognise the world isn't always going to be as it is now, so you need to be adaptable to the next wave in economics.

'And education, investment in education, those loop back into the conversation here. Don't forget, too, that there's always been a mercantile history in Cork, one that goes back a long, long time.

'To be fair to the businesses, to the business people and that community, they didn't take it lying down. They fought back through the chambers of commerce, all of that. That mercantile history, that tradition, allied to a sufficiency of movers and shakers who could devise clever strategic plans – that bore fruit in the medium to long term.

'It's a proud city. That's not being mawkish: Cork has achieved, in sporting terms, cultural terms, business terms. We're not going to lie down.

'There's no doubt the IDA was hugely helpful, with strategic investments in places like Ringaskiddy, we sometimes forget that. The land bank and utilities there meant the continued growth of the pharmaceutical industry, which has been there for fifty years and functions as a great steadying influence, even in the recent crash. But it was an intelligent comeback from the 1980s, and business people and others at the time were always prodding, meeting you with ideas, all that. There were always people with ideas.

'I remember Maurice Moloney, who was assistant city manager back then, saying to me, "God, Cork has fierce notions of 'wouldn't it be lovely if we had this'." There were always groups in to see him saying "we should do this" or "it would be lovely if we could do that."

'And the maritime influence is part of that, too, because I often think maritime communities are more open and creative because they come under influences from outside more often.'

A last word to Theo Dorgan.

'What stands out now? Confidence. And a certain kind of Cork pride, a specific pride and not a generalised "Cork, boy" but specific pride – specific to the Triskel growing, the Crawford, the National Sculpture Factory, the country's premier film festival, and we still had a hurling team, too.

'It became a tenet of international intellectual life that the local was important. But the local was how Cork lifted itself up. Through the 1970s Hibs were a serious team. Celtic were very good. We had serious hurlers. People had good steady jobs, and there was an equilibrium. Those jobs in Ford's, Dunlop's, Verolme, Irish Steel ... My Dad got a job in Dunlop's and was able to go to the County Council immediately and get a mortgage.

'Connolly used the term "the aristocracy of the working class", and Ford, Dunlop – those working there were a good credit risk because it was a job for life. A lot of the guys coming up to retirement, halfway through their mortgage – it was a desperate shock to them. It wasn't so much a shock to the city because I think even then the idea of a job for life was exotic. The transition was happening.

'The shock of those jobs going was considerable, but the children of those workers were in school. Some of them were in college – not enough of them, and still not enough of them – and some of those weren't interested in becoming wage slaves. They were exposed to eclectic influences and they wanted to follow those. What was happening in Detroit, that had repercussions in Cork.

'There was a great pride in Cork but it was a linked to specific achievements rather than a generalised "sure we're great". Something had to be done for someone to take pride in.'

Something was done. Cork came through.

Acknowledgements

've made no secret of the inspiration behind this book – *Once In A Great City* by David Maraniss, his magnificent account of a couple of crucial years in the history of Detroit. I was so blown away by Maraniss's accomplishment that nothing would do me but to try something similar.

Because of that I have to thank The Collins Press for their expertise, support and understanding, all of which made this a terrific experience.

I also thank the many people I interviewed for their patience and forbearance as I picked over the details of events now over three decades in the past. Your generosity is hugely appreciated, and it was a rare interview that finished without being given another person's name and number to chase up.

There were many others who were encouraging and constructive. Diarmuid O'Donovan nudged me in fruitful directions over many a coffee in Salt. Colm O'Callaghan made some key suggestions; he's been doing that for a long, long time.

Dave Hannigan reached across the Atlantic with a phone number. Ciaran McCarthy in the *Examiner* was always helpful, as was Tommy Barker. Eoin English went into his big book of telephone numbers for me.

My mother and father, Mary and Donal, are on the dedication page but they figure here as well. They kept us safe in a challenging time and brought us through: it is later one realises, as Bernard Spencer said.

Bobby and Breda Brennan were a huge support also in the writing of this book.

Marjorie facilitated me in this project as she has so often in the past: all my love for your understanding and support. Take on your own book next.

And Clara and Bridget: thanks for the light you guys shine on the cloudiest days. Sorry I didn't take your title suggestion on board, though 'Cork Before You Knew It' was definitely on the shortlist. I hope you enjoy the book when you get older. This is your home town.

Also from
The Collins Press

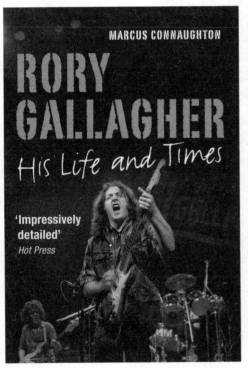

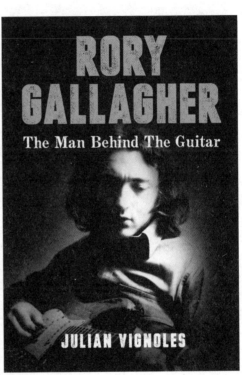

www.collinspress.ie

Also from
The Collins Press

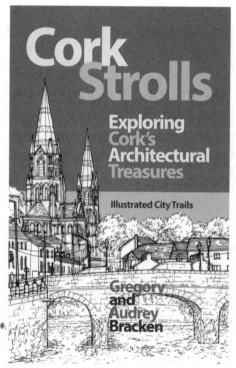

Also from
The Collins Press

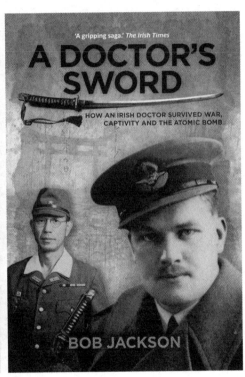

www.collinspress.ie

Also from
The Collins Press

www.collinspress.ie